BRITISH RAILWAYS

MULTIPLE UNITS

EIGHTEENTH EDITION
2005

The complete guide to all Diesel Multiple
Units which operate on National Rail

Robert Pritchard & Peter Fox

UPDATED TO 2007 EDITION 1.1.07

ISBN 1 902336 42 9

© 2004. Platform 5 Publishing Ltd., 3 Wyvern House, Sark Road, Sheffield,
S2 4HG, England.

POCKET

CONTENTS

PROVISION OF INFORMATION

This book has been compiled with care to be as accurate as possible, but in some cases official information is not available and the publisher cannot be held responsible for any errors or omissions. We would like to thank the companies and individuals which have been co-operative in supplying information to us. The authors of this series of books will be pleased to receive notification from readers of any inaccuracies readers may find in the series, and notification of any additional information to supplement our records and thus enhance future editions is always welcome. Please send comments to:

Robert Pritchard, Platform 5 Publishing Ltd., 3 Wyvern House, Sark Road, Sheffield, S2 4HG, England.
Tel: 0114 255 2625 **Fax**: 0114 255 2471
e-mail: Robert@platform5.com

Both the author and the staff of Platform 5 regret they are unable to answer specific queries regarding locomotives and rolling stock.

This book is updated to 8 November 2004.

UPDATES

An update to all the books in the *British Railways Pocket Book* series is published every month in the Platform 5 magazine, **entrain,** which contains news and rolling stock information on the railways of Britain and Ireland. For further details of **entrain,** please see the advertisement on the back cover of this book.

BRITAIN'S RAILWAY SYSTEM

INFRASTRUCTURE & OPERATION

Britain's national railway infrastructure is now owned by a "not for dividend" company, Network Rail. Many stations and maintenance depots are leased to and operated by Train Operating Companies (TOCs), but some larger stations remain under Network Rail control. The only exception is the infrastructure on the Isle of Wight, which is nationally owned and is leased to the Island Line franchisee.

Trains are operated by TOCs over Network Rail, regulated by access agreements between the parties involved. In general, TOCs are responsible for the provision and maintenance of the locomotives, rolling stock and staff necessary for the direct operation of services, whilst Network Rail is responsible for the provision and maintenance of the infrastructure and also for staff needed to regulate the operation of services.

DOMESTIC PASSENGER TRAIN OPERATORS

The large majority of passenger trains are operated by the TOCs on fixed term franchises. Franchise expiry dates are shown in parentheses in the list of franchisees below:

Franchise	Franchisee	Trading Name
Central Trains[1]	National Express Group plc (until 1 April 2006)	Central Trains
Chiltern Railways	M40 Trains Ltd. (until December 2021)	Chiltern Railways
Cross-Country[2]	Virgin Rail Group Ltd. (until further notice)	Virgin Trains
Gatwick Express[3]	National Express Group plc (until 27 April 2011)	Gatwick Express
Great Western Trains[4]	First Group plc (until 31 March 2006)	First Great Western
Greater Anglia[5]	National Express Group plc (until 31 March 2014)	"One"
InterCity East Coast[6]	GNER Holdings Ltd. (until 4 April 2005)	Great North Eastern Railway
InterCity West Coast	Virgin Rail Group Ltd. (until 8 March 2012)	Virgin Trains
Island Line	Stagecoach Holdings plc (until February 2007)	Island Line
LTS Rail	National Express Group plc (until 25 May 2011)	c2c
Merseyrail Electrics[7]	Serco/NedRail (until 20 July 2028)	Merseyrail Electrics

Midland Main Line	National Express Group plc (until 27 April 2008)	Midland Mainline
North London Railways	National Express Group plc (until 1 September 2006)	Silverlink Train Services
North West Regional Railways[8]	First Group plc (until 12 December 2004)	First North Western
Regional Railways North East[8]	Arriva Trains Ltd (until 12 December 2004)	Arriva Trains Northern
ScotRail	First Group plc (until 16 October 2011)	First ScotRail
South Central	GoVia Ltd. (Go-Ahead/Keolis). (until May 2010)	Southern
South Eastern[9]		South Eastern Trains
South West	Stagecoach Holdings plc (until 3 February 2007)	South West Trains
Thames[4]	First Group plc (until 31 March 2006)	First Great Western Link
Thameslink	GoVia Ltd. (until 1 April 2006)	Thameslink Rail
Trans-Pennine Express	First Group/Keolis (until 31 January 2012)	Trans-Pennine Express
Wales & Borders	Arriva Trains Ltd (until 6 December 2018)	Arriva Trains Wales
Wessex Trains[4]	National Express Group plc (until 31 March 2006)	Wessex Trains
Great Northern[10]	National Express Group plc (until 4 April 2006)	WAGN

Notes:

[1] Due to be abolished on expiry. Services expected to be split between Chiltern, Midland Mainline, Northern, Silverlink, and Cross-Country.

[2] At the time of going to press the future of this franchise was in doubt following its renegotiation, as the Strategic Rail Authority (SRA) then announced that Virgin's best and final offer for a single-tender deal running until 2012 did not represent value for money. The SRA has therefore told Virgin that it reserves the right to terminate the franchise.

[3] Gatwick Express has been proposed for possible absorption by Southern as part of the SRA's Brighton Main Line Route Utilisation Strategy. This could take place before the expiry of the current Gatwick Express franchise.

[4] Due to transfer to the new Greater Western franchise on 1 April 2006.

[5] Incorporates the former Anglia and Great Eastern franchises and the West Anglia half of West Anglia Great Northern.

[6] The preferred bidder for the new East Coast franchise is due to be announced in early 2005.

[7] Now under control of Merseyrail PTE instead of the SRA. Franchise due to be reviewed after seven years and then every five years to fit in with Merseyside Local Transport Plan.

[8] Urban and rural services currently run by Arriva Trains Northern and First North Western are due to transfer to the new Northern franchise on 12 December 2004, run by Serco/NedRail. Trans-Pennine services formerly run by these operators were taken over by the new Trans-Pennine Express franchise on 1 February 2004.

[9] New interim management company known as South Eastern Trains (SET) formed on 9 November 2003, pending award of new Integrated Kent franchise expected in early 2005. SET is a subsidiary of the SRA.

[10] The West Anglia half of WAGN transferred to new Greater Anglia franchise. The Great Northern half remains separate until its absorption by the new Thameslink franchise in 2006.

A major reorganisation of franchises is under way. See **entrain** for developments.

The following operators run non-franchised services only:

Operator	Trading Name	Route
British Airports Authority	Heathrow Express	London Paddington–Heathrow Airport
Hull Trains§	Hull Trains	London King's Cross–Hull
West Coast Railway Co.	West Coast Railway*	Birmingham Snow Hill–Stratford-on-Avon
		Fort William–Mallaig
		York–Scarborough

* Special summer-dated services only.
§ Now owned by First Group.

INTERNATIONAL PASSENGER OPERATIONS

Eurostar (UK) operates international passenger-only services between the United Kingdom and continental Europe, jointly with French National Railways (SNCF) and Belgian National Railways (SNCB/NMBS). Eurostar (UK) is a subsidiary of London & Continental Railways, which is jointly owned by National Express Group plc and British Airways.

In addition, a service for the conveyance of accompanied road vehicles through the Channel Tunnel is provided by the tunnel operating company, Eurotunnel.

FREIGHT TRAIN OPERATIONS

The following operators operate freight train services under "Open Access" arrangements:

English Welsh & Scottish Railway Ltd (EWS).
Freightliner Ltd.
GB Railfreight Ltd. (now owned by First Group)
Direct Rail Services Ltd.
Advenza Freight Ltd.

INTRODUCTION

DMU CLASSES

DMU Classes are listed in class number order. Principal details and dimensions are quoted for each class in metric and/or imperial units as considered appropriate bearing in mind common usage in the UK.

All dimensions and weights are quoted for vehicles in an "as new" condition with all necessary supplies (e.g. oil, water, sand) on board. Dimensions are quoted in the order Length – Width. All lengths quoted are over buffers or couplers as appropriate. All width dimensions quoted are maxima.

NUMERICAL LISTINGS

DMUs are listed in numerical order of set – using current numbers as allocated by the RSL. Individual 'loose' vehicles are listed in numerical order after vehicles formed into fixed formations. Where numbers carried are different from those officially allocated these are noted in class headings where appropriate. Where sets or vehicles have been renumbered in recent years, former numbering detail is shown in parentheses. Each entry is laid out as in the following example:

RSL Set No.	Detail	Livery	Owner	Operator	Depot	Formation		
142 080	v	**VL**	A	*AW*	CF	55730	55776	Caerphilly RFC

Detail Differences. Detail differences which currently affect the areas and types of train which vehicles may work are shown, plus differences in interior layout. Where such differences occur within a class, these are shown either in the heading information or alongside the individual set or vehicle number. The following standard abbreviation is used:

r   Radio Electronic Token Block (RETB) equipment.

In all cases use of the above abbreviations indicates the equipment indicated is normally operable. Meaning of non-standard abbreviations is detailed in individual class headings.

Set Formations. Regular set formations are shown where these are normally maintained. Readers should note set formations might be temporarily varied from time to time to suit maintenance and/or operational requirements. Vehicles shown as "spare" are not formed in any regular set formation.

Codes. Codes are used to denote the livery, owner, operation and depot of each unit. Details of these will be found in section 5 of this book. Where a unit or spare car is off-lease, the operation column will be left blank.

Names. Only names carried with official sanction are listed. As far as possible names are shown in UPPER/lower case characters as actually shown on the name carried on the vehicle(s). Unless otherwise shown, complete units are regarded as named rather than just the individual car(s) which carry the name.

GENERAL INFORMATION

CLASSIFICATION AND NUMBERING

First generation ("Heritage") DMUs are classified in the series 100–139.
Second generation DMUs are classified in the series 140–199.
Diesel-electric multiple units are classified in the series 200–249.
Service units are classified in the series 930–999.
First and second generation individual cars are numbered in the series 50000–59999 and 79000–79999.

DEMU individual cars are numbered in the series 60000–60999, except for a few former EMU vehicles which retain their EMU numbers.

Service stock individual cars are numbered in the series 975000–975999 and 977000–977999, although this series is not exclusively used for DMU vehicles.

OPERATING CODES

These codes are used by train operating company staff to describe the various different types of vehicles and normally appear on data panels on the inner (i.e. non driving) ends of vehicles.

The first part of the code describes whether or not the car has a motor or a driving cab as follows:

DM Driving motor.
M   Motor
DT Driving trailer
T   Trailer

The next letter is a "B" for cars with a brake compartment.

This is followed by the saloon details:

F   First
S   Standard
C   Composite
so denotes a semi-open vehicle (part compartments, part open). All other vehicles are assumed to consist solely of open saloons.

L denotes a vehicle with a lavatory compartment.

Finally vehicles with a buffet are suffixed RB or RMB for a miniature buffet.

Where two vehicles of the same type are formed within the same unit, the above codes may be suffixed by (A) and (B) to differentiate between the vehicles.

A composite is a vehicle containing both first and standard class accommodation, whilst a brake vehicle is a vehicle containing separate specific accommodation for the conductor.

Special Note: Where vehicles have been declassified, the correct operating code which describes the actual vehicle layout is quoted in this publication.

BUILD DETAILS

Lot Numbers

Vehicles ordered under the auspices of BR were allocated a Lot (batch) number when ordered and these are quoted in class headings and sub-headings.

ACCOMMODATION

The information given in class headings and sub-headings is in the form F/S nT (or TD) nW. For example 12/54 1T 1W denotes 12 first class and 54 standard class seats, one toilet and one space for a wheelchair. The seating layout of open saloons is shown as 2+1, 2+2 or 3+2 as the case may be. Where units have first class accommodation as well as standard and the layout is different for each class then these are shown separately prefixed by "1:" and "2:". Compartments are always three seats a side in first class and four a side in standard class in DMUs. TD denotes a toilet suitable for a disabled person.

ABBREVIATIONS

The following abbreviations are used in class headings and also throughout this publication:

BR	British Railways.
BSI	Bergische Stahl Industrie.
DEMU	Diesel electric multiple unit.
DMU	Diesel multiple unit (general term).
EMU	Electric multiple unit.
kN	kilonewtons.
km/h	kilometres per hour.
kW	kilowatts.
LT	London Transport.
LUL	London Underground Limited.
m.	metres.
m.p.h.	miles per hour.
t.	tonnes.

1. DIESEL MECHANICAL & DIESEL HYDRAULIC UNITS

FIRST GENERATION UNIT

CLASS 121   PRESSED STEEL SUBURBAN

First generation unit used by Chiltern Railways on selected Aylesbury–Princes Risborough services.
Construction: Steel.
Engines: Two Leyland 1595 of 112 kW (150 h.p.) at 1800 r.p.m.
Transmission: Mechanical. Cardan shaft and freewheel to a four-speed epicyclic gearbox and final drive.
Brakes: Vacuum.
Gangways: Non gangwayed single cars with cabs at each end.
Bogies: DD10.   **Couplers:** Screw couplings.
Dimensions: 20.45 x 2.82 m.   **Seating Layout:** 3+2 facing.
Doors: Manually-operated slam.   **Maximum Speed:** 70 m.p.h.
Multiple Working: "Blue Square" coupling code. First Generation vehicles cannot be coupled to Second Generation units.

55020. DMBS. Lot No. 30518 1960. –/65. 38.0 t.

Non-standard livery: 121 020 is all over Chiltern blue with a silver stripe.

Note: Also fitted with central door locking.

121 020   **0**   CR   *CR*   AL   55020

SECOND GENERATION UNITS

All units in this section have air brakes and are equipped with public address, with transmission equipment on driving vehicles and flexible diaphragm gangways. Except where otherwise stated, transmission is Voith 211r hydraulic with a cardan shaft to a Gmeinder GM190 final drive.

CLASS 142   PACER   BREL DERBY/LEYLAND

DMS–DMSL.

Construction: Steel. Built from Leyland National bus parts on four-wheeled underframes.
Engines: One Cummins LTA10-R of 172 kW (230 h.p.) at 2100 r.p.m.
(* One Perkins 2006-TWH of 172 kW (230 h.p.) at 2100 r.p.m.).
Couplers: BSI at outer ends, bar within unit.
Seating Layout: 3+2 mainly unidirectional bus/bench style unless stated.
Dimensions: 15.66 x 2.80 m.
Gangways: Within unit only.   **Wheel Arrangement:** 1-A A-1.
Doors: Twin-leaf inward pivoting.   **Maximum Speed:** 75 m.p.h.
Multiple Working: Within class and with Classes 143, 144, 150, 153, 155, 156, 158, 159.

55542–55591. DMS. Lot No. 31003 1985–1986. –/62 (s –/56, t –/53 or 55 1W, u –/52 or 54 1W, v –/52 1W) 23.26 t.
55592–55641. DMSL. Lot No. 31004 1985–1986. –/59 1T (s –/50 1T, u –/60 1T, v –/50 1T) 24.97 t.
55701–55746. DMS. Lot No. 31013 1986–1987. –/62 (s –/56, t –/53 or 55 1W, u –/52 or 54 1W, v –/52 1W) 23.26 t.
55747–55792. DMSL. Lot No. 31014 1986–1987. –/59 1T (s –/50 1T, u –/60 1T, v–/50 1T) 24.97 t.

s Fitted with 2+2 individual high-backed seating.
t First North Western facelifted units – DMS fitted with luggage rack and wheelchair space.
u Merseytravel units – Fitted with 3+2 individual low-back seating.
v Refurbished Arriva Trains Wales units. Fitted with 2+2 individual Chapman seating.

142 001	t	**NW**	A	*NW*	NH	55542	55592
142 002	v	**VL**	A	*AW*	CF	55543	55593
142 003	t	**NW**	A	*NW*	NH	55544	55594
142 004	t	**NW**	A	*NW*	NH	55545	55595
142 005	t	**NW**	A	*NW*	NH	55546	55596
142 006	v	**VL**	A	*AW*	CF	55547	55597
142 007	t	**NW**	A	*NW*	NH	55548	55598
142 009	t	**NW**	A	*NW*	NH	55550	55600	Newton Heath 125 1876–2001
142 010	v	**VL**	A	*AW*	CF	55551	55601
142 011	t	**NW**	A	*NW*	NH	55552	55602
142 012	t	**NW**	A	*NW*	NH	55553	55603

142 013	t	**NW**	A	*NW*	NH	55554	55604
142 014	t	**NW**	A	*NW*	NH	55555	55605
142 015	s	**AV**	A	*AN*	HT	55556	55606
142 016	s	**AV**	A	*AN*	HT	55557	55607
142 017	s	**AV**	A	*AN*	HT	55558	55608
142 018	s	**AV**	A	*AN*	HT	55559	55609
142 019	s	**AV**	A	*AN*	HT	55560	55610
142 020	s	**AV**	A	*AN*	HT	55561	55611
142 021	s	**AV**	A	*AN*	HT	55562	55612
142 022	s	**AV**	A	*AN*	HT	55563	55613
142 023	t	**NW**	A	*NW*	NH	55564	55614
142 024	s	**AV**	A	*AN*	HT	55565	55615
142 025	s	**NS**	A	*AN*	HT	55566	55616
142 026	s	**AV**	A	*AN*	HT	55567	55617
142 027	t	**NW**	A	*NW*	NH	55568	55618
142 028	t	**NW**	A	*NW*	NH	55569	55619
142 029	t	**NW**	A	*NW*	NH	55570	55620
142 030	t	**NW**	A	*NW*	NH	55571	55621
142 031	t	**NW**	A	*NW*	NH	55572	55622
142 032	t	**NW**	A	*NW*	NH	55573	55623
142 033	t	**NW**	A	*NW*	NH	55574	55624
142 034	t	**NW**	A	*NW*	NH	55575	55625
142 035	t	**NW**	A	*NW*	NH	55576	55626
142 036	t	**NW**	A	*NW*	NH	55577	55627
142 037	t	**NW**	A	*NW*	NH	55578	55628
142 038	t	**NW**	A	*NW*	NH	55579	55629
142 039	t	**NS**	A	*NW*	NH	55580	55630
142 040	t	**NW**	A	*NW*	NH	55581	55631
142 041	u	**MY**	A	*NW*	NH	55582	55632
142 042	u	**MY**	A	*NW*	NH	55583	55633
142 043	u	**MY**	A	*NW*	NH	55584	55634
142 044	u	**MY**	A	*NW*	NH	55585	55635
142 045	u	**MY**	A	*NW*	NH	55586	55636
142 046	u	**MY**	A	*NW*	NH	55587	55637
142 047	u	**MY**	A	*NW*	NH	55588	55638
142 048	u	**MY**	A	*NW*	NH	55589	55639
142 049	u	**MY**	A	*NW*	NH	55590	55640
142 050	s	**NS**	A	*AN*	HT	55591	55641
142 051	u	**MY**	A	*NW*	NH	55701	55747
142 052	u	**MY**	A	*NW*	NH	55702	55748
142 053	u	**MY**	A	*NW*	NH	55703	55749
142 054	u	**MY**	A	*NW*	NH	55704	55750
142 055	u	**MY**	A	*NW*	NH	55705	55751
142 056	u	**MY**	A	*NW*	NH	55706	55752
142 057	u	**MY**	A	*NW*	NH	55707	55753
142 058	u	**MY**	A	*NW*	NH	55708	55754
142 060	t	**NW**	A	*NW*	NH	55710	55756
142 061	t	**NW**	A	*NW*	NH	55711	55757
142 062	t	**NW**	A	*NW*	NH	55712	55758
142 063	t	**NW**	A	*NW*	NH	55713	55759
142 064	t	**NW**	A	*NW*	NH	55714	55760

142 065	s	**NS**	A	*AN*	HT	55715	55761
142 066	s	**NS**	A	*AN*	HT	55716	55762
142 067	t	**NW**	A	*NW*	NH	55717	55763
142 068	t	**NW**	A	*NW*	NH	55718	55764
142 069	v	**VL**	A	*AW*	CF	55719	55765
142 070	t	**NW**	A	*NW*	NH	55720	55766
142 071	s	**AV**	A	*AN*	HT	55721	55767
142 072	v	**VL**	A	*AW*	CF	55722	55768
142 073	v	**VL**	A	*AW*	CF	55723	55769	Myfanwy
142 074	v	**VL**	A	*AW*	CF	55724	55770
142 075	v	**VL**	A	*AW*	CF	55725	55771
142 076	v	**VL**	A	*AW*	CF	55726	55772
142 077	v	**VL**	A	*AW*	CF	55727	55773
142 078	s	**AV**	A	*AN*	HT	55728	55774
142 079	s	**AV**	A	*AN*	HT	55729	55775
142 080	v	**VL**	A	*AW*	CF	55730	55776	Caerphilly R.F.C.
142 081	v	**VW**	A	*AW*	CF	55731	55777
142 082	v	**VL**	A	*AW*	CF	55732	55778
142 083	v	**VL**	A	*AW*	CF	55733	55779
142 084	s*	**AV**	A	*AN*	HT	55734	55780
142 085	v	**VL**	A	*AW*	CF	55735	55781
142 086	s	**AV**	A	*AN*	HT	55736	55782
142 087	s	**AV**	A	*AN*	HT	55737	55783
142 088	s	**AV**	A	*AN*	HT	55738	55784
142 089	s	**AV**	A	*AN*	HT	55739	55785
142 090	s	**AV**	A	*AN*	HT	55740	55786
142 091	s	**AV**	A	*AN*	HT	55741	55787
142 092	s	**AV**	A	*AN*	HT	55742	55788
142 093	s	**AV**	A	*AN*	HT	55743	55789
142 094	s	**AV**	A	*AN*	HT	55744	55790
142 095	s	**AV**	A	*AN*	HT	55745	55791
142 096	s	**AV**	A	*AN*	HT	55746	55792

CLASS 143   PACER   ALEXANDER/BARCLAY

DMS–DMSL. Similar design to Class 142, but bodies built by W. Alexander with Barclay underframes.

Construction: Steel. Alexander bus bodywork on four-wheeled underframes.
Engines: One Cummins LTA10-R of 172 kW (230 h.p.) at 2100 r.p.m.
Couplers: BSI at outer ends, bar couplers within unit.
Seating Layout: All units are now fitted with 2+2 high-back Chapman seating, mainly unidirectional.
Dimensions: 15.55 x 2.70 m.
Gangways: Within unit only.   **Wheel Arrangement:** 1-A A-1.
Doors: Twin-leaf inward pivoting.   **Maximum Speed:** 75 m.p.h.
Multiple Working: Within class and with Classes 142, 144, 150, 153, 155, 156, 158, 159.

DMS. Lot No. 31005 Andrew Barclay 1985–1986. –/54. 24.5 t.
DMSL. Lot No. 31006 Andrew Barclay 1985–1986. –/50 1T. 25.0 t.

143 601	**VL**	RD	*AW*	CF	55642	55667	
143 602	**VL**	P	*AW*	CF	55651	55668	
143 603	**BI**	P	*WX*	EX	55658	55669	
143 604	**VL**	P	*AW*	CF	55645	55670	
143 605	**VL**	P	*AW*	CF	55646	55671	Crimestoppers
143 606	**VL**	P	*AW*	CF	55647	55672	
143 607	**VL**	P	*AW*	CF	55648	55673	
143 608	**VL**	P	*AW*	CF	55649	55674	
143 609	**VL**	BC	*AW*	CF	55650	55675	Tom Jones
143 610	**VL**	RD	*AW*	CF	55643	55676	
143 611	**BI**	P	*WX*	EX	55652	55677	
143 612	**BI**	P	*WX*	EX	55653	55678	
143 613	**BI**	P		PM	55654	55679	
143 614	**VL**	RD	*AW*	CF	55655	55680	
143 615	**VL**	P		CF	55656	55681	
143 616	**VL**	P	*AW*	CF	55657	55682	
143 617	**BI**	RI	*WX*	EX	55644	55683	
143 618	**BI**	RI	*WX*	EX	55659	55684	
143 619	**BI**	RI	*WX*	EX	55660	55685	
143 620	**BI**	P	*WX*	EX	55661	55686	
143 621	**BI**	P	*WX*	EX	55662	55687	
143 622	**BI**	P	*AW*	CF	55663	55688	
143 623	**BI**	P	*AW*	CF	55664	55689	
143 624	**VL**	P	*AW*	CF	55665	55690	
143 625	**VL**	P	*AW*	CF	55666	55691	Valleys Kids

CLASS 144   PACER   ALEXANDER/BREL DERBY

DMS–DMSL or DMS–MS–DMSL. As Class 143, but underframes built by BREL.

Construction: Steel. Alexander bus bodywork on four-wheeled underframes.
Engines: One Cummins LTA10-R of 172 kW (230 h.p.) at 2100 r.p.m.
Couplers: BSI at outer ends, bar couplers within unit.
Seating Layout: All units now fitted with 2+2 high-back Richmond seating, mainly unidirectional.
Dimensions: 15.55 x 2.73 m.
Gangways: Within unit only.   **Wheel Arrangement:** 1-A A-1.
Doors: Twin-leaf inward pivoting.   **Maximum Speed:** 75 m.p.h.
Multiple Working: Within class and with Classes 142, 143, 150, 153, 155, 156, 158, 159.

DMS. Lot No. 31015 BREL Derby 1986–1987. –/48 1W 24.2 t.
MS. Lot No. BREL Derby 31037 1987. –/58 22.6 t.
DMSL. Lot No. BREL Derby 31016 1986–1987. –/45 1T 25.0 t.

Notes: The centre cars of the 3-car units are owned by West Yorkshire PTE, although managed by Porterbrook Leasing Company.

144 001	**YP**	P	*AN*	NL	55801		55824
144 002	**YP**	P	*AN*	NL	55802		55825
144 003	**YP**	P	*AN*	NL	55803		55826
144 004	**YP**	P	*AN*	NL	55804		55827
144 005	**YP**	P	*AN*	NL	55805		55828
144 006	**YP**	P	*AN*	NL	55806		55829
144 007	**YP**	P	*AN*	NL	55807		55830
144 008	**YP**	P	*AN*	NL	55808		55831
144 009	**YP**	P	*AN*	NL	55809		55832
144 010	**YP**	P	*AN*	NL	55810		55833
144 011	**YP**	P	*AN*	NL	55811		55834
144 012	**YP**	P	*AN*	NL	55812		55835
144 013	**YP**	P	*AN*	NL	55813		55836
144 014	**YP**	P	*AN*	NL	55814	55850	55837
144 015	**YP**	P	*AN*	NL	55815	55851	55838
144 016	**YP**	P	*AN*	NL	55816	55852	55839
144 017	**YP**	P	*AN*	NL	55817	55853	55840
144 018	**YP**	P	*AN*	NL	55818	55854	55841
144 019	**YP**	P	*AN*	NL	55819	55855	55842
144 020	**YP**	P	*AN*	NL	55820	55856	55843
144 021	**YP**	P	*AN*	NL	55821	55857	55844
144 022	**YP**	P	*AN*	NL	55822	55858	55845
144 023	**YP**	P	*AN*	NL	55823	55859	55846

Name (carried on DMSL): 144 001 THE PENISTONE LINE PARTNERSHIP

CLASS 150/0   SPRINTER   BREL YORK

DMSL–MS–DMS. Prototype Sprinter.

Construction: Steel.
Engines: One Cummins NT-855-R4 of 213 kW (285 h.p.) at 2100 r.p.m.
Bogies: BX8P (powered), BX8T (non-powered).
Couplers: BSI at outer end of driving vehicles, bar non-driving ends.
Seating Layout: 3+2 (mainly unidirectional).
Dimensions: 20.06/20.18 x 2.82 m.
Gangways: Within unit only.   **Wheel Arrangement:** 2-B – 2-B – B-2.
Doors: Twin-leaf sliding.   **Maximum Speed:** 75 m.p.h.
Multiple Working: Within class and with Classes 142, 143, 144, 153, 155, 156, 158, 159, 170.

DMSL. Lot No. 30984 1984. –/72 1T. 35.8 t.
MS. Lot No. 30986 1984. –/92. 34.4 t.
DMS. Lot No. 30985 1984. –/76. 35.6 t.

150 001	r	**CO**	A	*CT*	TS	55200	55400	55300
150 002	r	**CO**	A	*CT*	TS	55201	55401	55301

CLASS 150/1   SPRINTER   BREL YORK

DMSL–DMS or DMSL–DMSL–DMS or DMSL–DMS–DMS.

Construction: Steel.
Engines: One Cummins NT855R5 of 213 kW (285 h.p.) at 2100 r.p.m.
Bogies: BP38 (powered), BT38 (non-powered).
Couplers: BSI.
Seating Layout: 3+2 facing as built but Centro units were reseated with mainly unidirectional seating.
Dimensions: 19.74 x 2.82 m.
Gangways: Within unit only.   **Wheel Arrangement:** 2-B (– 2–B) – B-2.
Doors: Twin-leaf sliding.   **Maximum Speed:** 75 m.p.h.
Multiple Working: Within class and with Classes 142, 143, 144, 153, 155, 156, 158, 159, 170.

DMSL. Lot No. 31011 1985–1986. –/72 1T (s –/59 1TD, t –/71 1W 1T, u –/71 1T). 36.5 t.
DMS. Lot No. 31012 1985–1986. –/76 (s –/65, u –/70). 38.45 t.

Non-standard livery: 150 134 is in plain dark blue.

Notes: The centre cars of 3-car units are Class 150/2 vehicles. For details see Class 150/2.
Units in **NW** livery have been refurbished with new Chapman seating.

150 003	ru	**CO**	A	*CT*	TS	52103	57210	57103
150 004	ru	**CO**	A	*CT*	TS	52104	52216	57104
150 005	ru	**CO**	A	*CT*	TS	52105	52210	57105
150 006	ru	**CO**	A	*CT*	TS	52106	57214	57106
150 008	ru	**CO**	A	*CT*	TS	52108	57216	57108
150 010	ru	**CO**	A	*CT*	TS	52110	57226	57110
150 011	ru	**CO**	A	*CT*	TS	52111	52204	57111
150 012	ru	**CO**	A	*CT*	TS	52112	57206	57112
150 013	ru	**CO**	A	*CT*	TS	52113	52226	57113
150 014	ru	**CO**	A	*CT*	TS	52114	57204	57114
150 015	ru	**CO**	A	*CT*	TS	52115	52206	57115
150 016	ru	**CO**	A	*CT*	TS	52116	57212	57116
150 017	ru	**CO**	A	*CT*	TS	52117	57209	57117
150 018	ru	**CO**	A	*CT*	TS	52118	57220	57118
150 019	ru	**CO**	A	*CT*	TS	52119	57220	57119
150 022	ru	**CO**	A	*CT*	TS	52122	52214	57122
150 101	ru	**CO**	A	*CT*	TS	52101	57101	
150 102	ru	**CO**	A	*CT*	TS	52102	57102	
150 107	r	**CO**	A	*CT*	TS	52107	57107	
150 109	ru	**CO**	A	*CT*	TS	52109	57109	
150 120	t	**SL**	A	*SL*	BY	52120	57120	Gospel Oak–Barking 2000
150 121	ru	**CO**	A	*CT*	TS	52121	57121	
150 123	t	**SL**	A	*SL*	BY	52123	57123	Bletchley Seven
150 124	ru	**CO**	A	*CT*	TS	52124	57124	

▲ North Western Trains-liveried 142 014 approaches Grindleford with the 10.43 Manchester–Sheffield stopping service on 17/03/03. **George Allsop**

▼ Refurbished 3-car Class 144 in the new West Yorkshire PTE "Metro" livery 144 019 passes Mirfield with a Leeds–Huddersfield service on 29/05/04.

Gavin Morrison

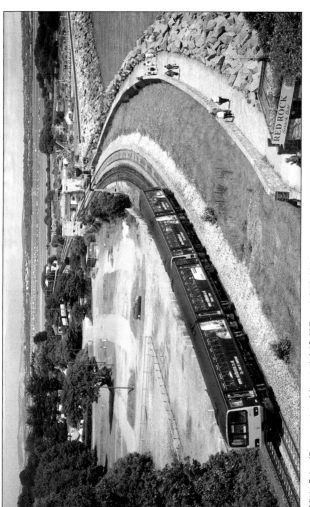

"Visit Bristol" promotional-liveried 143 617 and 143 620 are seen on 10/07/04 leaving Dawlish Warren with the 09.15 Cardiff–Paignton. **Robert Pritchard**

▲ The prototype Class 150 No. 150 001; 21 years old in 2005, passes Cossington, Leicestershire with the 11.41 Lincoln–Shrewsbury on 16/07/03. **Chris Booth**

▼ "Visit Wales" promotional liveried 150 281 and 153 312 are seen at Whitland on 09/08/03 with the 12.16 Pembroke Dock–Swansea service. **Gavin Morrison**

▲ Devon/Cornwall promotional-liveried 153 308 departs Southampton Central on 24/05/04 with a service to Swindon. **Mervyn Turvey**

▼ Old West Yorkshire PTE-liveried 155 346 passes Stourton on 25/02/04 with the 12.04 Leeds–Castleford service. **Jason Rogers**

▲ 156 410 in Central Trains livery passes Longport on 18/05/04 with a Skegness–Crewe service. **Cliff Beeton**

▼ Strathclyde carmine & cream-liveried 156 442 passes Greenhill Lower Junction with the 17.59 Falkirk Grahamston–Glasgow Queen Street on 17/08/04. **Ian Lothian**

ScotRail-liveried 158 728 passes Larbert with the 08.41 Dunblane–Glasgow Queen Street on 05/06/04. **Ian Lothian**

▲ Wessex Trains-liveried 158 869 enters Liskeard with the 10.20 Penzance–Bristol on 15/05/04. **Jonathan Allen**

▼ South West Trains-liveried 159 009 leads a 6-car formation through Lancing with the 07.08 Salisbury–Brighton on 20/09/03. **Alex Dasi-Sutton**

Chiltern Railways-liveried 165 024 leads a 6-car formation near Banbury with a Birmingham–Marylebone service on 02/06/04.

Jason Rogers

150 125	ru	CO	A	CT	TS	52125 57125	
150 126	ru	CO	A	CT	TS	52126 57126	
150 127	t	SL	A	SL	BY	52127 57127	Bletchley TMD
150 128	t	SL	A	SL	BY	52128 57128	Community Forest
150 129	t	SL	A	SL	BY	52129 57129	MARSTON VALE
150 130	t	SL	A	SL	BY	52130 57130	Bedford–Bletchley 150
150 131	t	SL	A	SL	BY	52131 57131	LESLIE CRABBE
150 132	r	CO	A	CT	TS	52132 57132	
150 133	s	NW	A	NW	NH	52133 57133	
150 134	s	O	A	NW	NH	52134 57134	
150 135	s	NW	A	NW	NH	52135 57135	
150 136	s	NW	A	NW	NH	52136 57136	
150 137	s	NW	A	NW	NH	52137 57137	
150 138	s	NW	A	NW	NH	52138 57138	
150 139	s	NW	A	NW	NH	52139 57139	
150 140	s	NW	A	NW	NH	52140 57140	
150 141	s	NW	A	NW	NH	52141 57141	
150 142	s	NW	A	NW	NH	52142 57142	
150 143	s	NW	A	NW	NH	52143 57143	
150 144	s	NW	A	NW	NH	52144 57144	
150 145	s	NW	A	NW	NH	52145 57145	
150 146	s	NW	A	NW	NH	52146 57146	
150 147	s	NW	A	NW	NH	52147 57147	
150 148	s	NW	A	NW	NH	52148 57148	
150 149	s	NW	A	NW	NH	52149 57149	
150 150	s	NW	A	NW	NH	52150 57150	

CLASS 150/2   SPRINTER   BREL YORK

DMSL–DMS.

Construction: Steel.
Engines: One Cummins NT855R5 of 213 kW (285 h.p.) at 2100 r.p.m.
Bogies: BP38 (powered), BT38 (non-powered).
Couplers: BSI.
Seating Layout: 3+2 mainly unidirectional seating as built, but many units have now been refurbished with 2+2 seating.
Dimensions: 19.74 x 2.82 m.
Gangways: Throughout.   **Wheel Arrangement:** 2-B – B-2.
Doors: Twin-leaf sliding.   **Maximum Speed:** 75 m.p.h.
Multiple Working: Within class and with Classes 142, 143, 144, 153, 155, 156, 158, 159, 170.

DMSL. Lot No. 31017 1986–1987. –/73 1T (s –/62 1TD, v –/68 1T, w –/68 1T). 35.8 t.
DMS. Lot No. 31018 1986–1987. –/76 (* –/68, s –/70, v –/71, w –/73). 34.9 t.

Notes: Units in NW livery have been refurbished with Chapman seating.
v Refurbished Arriva Trains Wales units with 2+2 individual Chapman seating.
w Refurbished Wessex Trains units with 2+2 individual Chapman seating.
One Anglia units have Chapman seating.

150 201	s	NW	A	NW	NH	52201	57201	
150 202		CO	A	CT	TS	52202	57202	
150 203	s	NW	A	NW	NH	52203	57203	
150 205	s	NW	A	NW	NH	52205	57205	
150 207	s	NW	A	NW	NH	52207	57207	
150 208		SR	P	SR	HA	52208	57208	
150 211	s	NW	A	NW	NH	52211	57211	
150 213	r*	AR	P	1A	NC	52213	57213	LORD NELSON
150 215	s	NW	A	NW	NH	52215	57215	
150 217	r*	AR	P	1A	NC	52217	57217	OLIVER CROMWELL
150 218	s	NW	A	NW	NH	52218	57218	
150 219	rw	WZ	P	WX	EX	52219	57219	
150 221	rw	WZ	P	WX	EX	52221	57221	
150 222	s	NW	A	NW	NH	52222	57222	
150 223	s	NW	A	NW	NH	52223	57223	
150 224	s	NW	A	NW	NH	52224	57224	
150 225	s	NW	A	NW	NH	52225	57225	
150 227	r*	AR	P	1A	NC	52227	57227	SIR ALF RAMSEY
150 228	tu	RR	P	AN	NL	52228	57228	
150 229	r*	AR	P	1A	NC	52229	57229	GEORGE BORROW
150 230	rw	WZ	P	WX	EX	52230	57230	The Tamar Kingfisher
150 231	r*	AR	P	1A	NC	52231	57231	KING EDMUND
150 232	rw	WZ	P	WX	EX	52232	57232	The Coastal Connection
150 233	rw	WZ	P	WX	EX	52233	57233	The Lady Margaret of Looe Valley
150 234	rw	WZ	P	WX	EX	52234	57234	The National Trust
150 235	r*	AR	P	1A	NC	52235	57235	CARDINAL WOLSEY
150 236	rw	WZ	P	WX	EX	52236	57236	The Lord Clinton
150 237	r*	AR	P	1A	NC	52237	57237	HEREWARD THE WAKE
150 238	rw	WZ	P	WX	EX	52238	57238	Exeter Explorer
150 239	rw	WZ	P	WX	EX	52239	57239	
150 240	rw	WZ	P	WX	EX	52240	57240	
150 241	rw	WZ	P	WX	EX	52241	57241	The Tarka Belle
150 242	rw	WZ	P	WX	EX	52242	57242	
150 243	rw	WZ	P	WX	EX	52243	57243	The Filton Partnership
150 244	rw	WZ	P	WX	EX	52244	57244	The West Cornwall Experience
150 245	r	AR	P	1A	NC	52245	57245	
150 246	rw	WZ	P	WX	EX	52246	57246	
150 247	rw	WZ	P	WX	EX	52247	57247	
150 248	rw	WZ	P	WX	EX	52248	57248	The Great Gardens of Cornwall
150 249	rw	WZ	P	WX	EX	52249	57249	
150 250		SR	P	SR	HA	52250	57250	
150 251	rw	WZ	P	WX	EX	52251	57251	
150 252		SR	P	SR	HA	52252	57252	
150 253	rw	WZ	P	WX	EX	52253	57253	The Exmouth Avocet
150 254	rw	WZ	P	WX	EX	52254	57254	
150 255	r*	AR	P	1A	NC	52255	57255	HENRY BLOGG
150 256		SR	P	SR	HA	52256	57256	
150 257	r*	AR	P	1A	NC	52257	57257	QUEEN BOADICEA

150 258		**SR**	P	*SR*	HA	52258	57258
150 259		**SR**	P	*SR*	HA	52259	57259
150 260		**SR**	P	*SR*	HA	52260	57260
150 261	rw	**WZ**	P	*WX*	EX	52261	57261	The Riviera Flyer
150 262		**SR**	P	*SR*	HA	52262	57262
150 263	rw	**WZ**	P	*WX*	EX	52263	57263	The Castles of Cornwall
150 264		**SR**	P	*SR*	HA	52264	57264
150 265	rw	**WZ**	P	*WX*	EX	52265	57265	The Falmouth Flyer
150 266	rw	**WZ**	P	*WX*	EX	52266	57266	The Whitley Wonder
150 267	rv	**VW**	P	*AW*	CF	52267	57267
150 268		**RR**	P	*AN*	NL	52268	57268
150 269		**RR**	P	*AN*	NL	52269	57269
150 270		**RR**	P	*AN*	NL	52270	57270
150 271		**RR**	P	*AN*	NL	52271	57271
150 272		**RR**	P	*AN*	NL	52272	57272
150 273		**RR**	P	*AN*	NL	52273	57273
150 274		**RR**	P	*AN*	NL	52274	57274
150 275		**RR**	P	*AN*	NL	52275	57275
150 276		**RR**	P	*AN*	NL	52276	57276
150 277		**RR**	P	*AN*	NL	52277	57277
150 278	rv	**VW**	P	*AW*	CF	52278	57278
150 279	v	**VW**	P	*AW*	CF	52279	57279
150 280	v	**VW**	P	*AW*	CF	52280	57280	University of Glamorgan/ Prifysgol Morgannwg
150 281	v	**VW**	P	*AW*	CF	52281	57281
150 282	v	**VW**	P	*AW*	CF	52282	57282
150 283		**SR**	P	*SR*	HA	52283	57283
150 284		**SR**	P	*SR*	HA	52284	57284
150 285		**SR**	P	*SR*	HA	52285	57285	EDINBURGH BATHGATE 1986–1996

CLASS 153   SUPER SPRINTER   LEYLAND BUS

DMSL. Converted by Hunslet-Barclay, Kilmarnock from Class 155 2-car units.

Construction: Steel. Built from Leyland National bus parts on bogied underframes.
Engine: One Cummins NT855R5 of 213 kW (285 h.p.) at 2100 r.p.m.
Bogies: One P3-10 (powered) and one BT38 (non-powered).
Couplers: BSI.
Seating Layout: 2+2 facing/unidirectional.
Dimensions: 23.21 x 2.70 m.
Gangways: Throughout.   **Wheel Arrangement:** 2-B.
Doors: Single-leaf sliding plug.   **Maximum Speed:** 75 m.p.h.
Multiple Working: Within class and with Classes 142, 143, 144, 150, 155, 156, 158, 159, 170.

52301–52335. DMSL. Lot No. 31026 1987–1988. Converted under Lot No.31115 1991–2. –/75 1T 1W (* –/69 1T 1W). 41.2 t.
57301–57335. DMSL. Lot No. 31027 1987–1988. Converted under Lot No.31115 1991–2. –/75 1T (* –/69 1T). 41.2 t.

Advertising Livery: 153 314 Norfolk and Norwich Festival (Black and orange).

Notes: Cars numbered in the 573xx series were renumbered by adding 50 to their original number so that the last two digits correspond with the set number. Central Trains and First North Western units have been fitted with Chapman seating.
Arriva Trains Northern units have been fitted with new Richmond seating.
Arriva Trains Wales/Wessex Trains units have been reseated with seats removed from that company's Class 158 units.
One Anglia units have Chapman seating and a bicycle rack.

153 301		AV	A	AN	NL	52301
153 302	r	DC	A	WX	EX	52302
153 303	r	HW	A	AW	CF	52303
153 304		AV	A	AN	NL	52304
153 305	r	WX	A	WX	EX	52305
153 306	r*	PS	P	1A	NC	52306	EDITH CAVELL
153 307		AV	A	AN	NL	52307
153 308	r	DC	A	WX	EX	52308
153 309	r*	AR	P	1A	NC	52309	GERARD FIENNES
153 310	r	NW	P	AW	CF	52310
153 311	r*	PS	P	1A	NC	52311	JOHN CONSTABLE
153 312	r	HW	A	AW	CF	52312
153 313	r	NW	P	AW	CF	52313
153 314	r*	AL	P	1A	NC	52314	DELIA SMITH
153 315		AV	A	AN	NL	52315
153 316		NW	P	NW	NH	52316
153 317		AV	A	AN	NL	52317
153 318	r	WX	A	WX	EX	52318
153 319		AV	A	AN	NL	52319
153 320	r	HW	P	AW	CF	52320
153 321	r	HW	P	AW	CF	52321
153 322	r*	AR	P	1A	NC	52322	BENJAMIN BRITTEN
153 323	r	HW	P	AW	CF	52323
153 324		NW	P	NW	NH	52324
153 325	r	RR	P	CT	TS	52325
153 326	r*	PS	P	1A	NC	52326	TED ELLIS
153 327	r	HW	A	AW	CF	52327
153 328		AV	A	AN	NL	52328
153 329	r	RR	P	WX	EX	52329
153 330		NW	P	NW	NH	52330
153 331		AV	A	AN	NL	52331
153 332		NW	P	NW	NH	52332
153 333	r	CT	P	CT	TS	52333
153 334	r	CT	P	CT	TS	52334
153 335	r*	AR	P	1A	NC	52335	MICHAEL PALIN
153 351		AV	A	AN	NL	57351
153 352		AV	A	AN	NL	57352
153 353	r	HW	A	AW	CF	57353
153 354	r	CT	P	CT	TS	57354
153 355	r	WX	A	WX	EX	57355
153 356	r	RR	P	CT	TS	57356

153 357		AV	A	AN	NL	57357
153 358		NW	P	NW	NH	57358
153 359		NW	P	NW	NH	57359
153 360		NW	P	NW	NH	57360
153 361	r	NW	P	AW	CF	57361
153 362	r	HW	A	AW	CF	57362
153 363		NW	P	NW	NH	57363
153 364	r	RR	P	CT	TS	57364
153 365	r	CT	P	CT	TS	57365
153 366	r	RR	P	CT	TS	57366
153 367	r	NW	P	AW	CF	57367
153 368	r	WX	A	WX	EX	57368
153 369	r	RR	P	WX	EX	57369
153 370	r	WX	A	WX	EX	57370
153 371	r	CT	P	CT	TS	57371
153 372	r	WX	A	WX	EX	57372
153 373	r	WX	A	WX	EX	57373
153 374	r	DC	A	WX	EX	57374
153 375	r	CT	P	CT	TS	57375
153 376	r	RR	P	CT	TS	57376
153 377	r	DC	A	WX	EX	57377
153 378		AV	A	AN	NL	57378
153 379	r	RR	P	CT	TS	57379
153 380	r	DC	A	WX	EX	57380
153 381	r	CT	P	CT	TS	57381
153 382	r	DC	A	WX	EX	57382
153 383	r	CT	P	CT	TS	57383
153 384	r	RR	P	CT	TS	57384
153 385	r	CT	P	CT	TS	57385

Dylan Thomas 1914–1953

CLASS 155   SUPER SPRINTER   LEYLAND BUS

DMSL–DMS.

Construction: Steel. Built from Leyland National bus parts on bogied underframes.
Engines: One Cummins NT855R5 of 213 kW (285 h.p.) at 2100 r.p.m.
Bogies: One P3-10 (powered) and one BT38 (non-powered).
Couplers: BSI.
Seating Layout: 2+2 facing/unidirectional.
Dimensions: 23.21 x 2.70 m.
Gangways: Throughout.
Doors: Single-leaf sliding plug.
Multiple Working: Within class and with Classes 142, 143, 144, 150, 153, 156, 158, 159, 170.

Wheel Arrangement: 2-B – B-2.
Maximum Speed: 75 m.p.h.

DMSL. Lot No. 31057 1988. –/80 1TD 1W. 39.0 t.
DMS. Lot No. 31058 1988. –/80. 38.7 t.

Note: These units are owned by West Yorkshire PTE, although managed by Porterbrook Leasing Company.

155 341	**WY**	P	*AN*	NL	52341	57341
155 342	**WY**	P	*AN*	NL	52342	57342
155 343	**WY**	P	*AN*	NL	52343	57343
155 344	**WY**	P	*AN*	NL	52344	57344
155 345	**WY**	P	*AN*	NL	52345	57345
155 346	**WY**	P	*AN*	NL	52346	57346
155 347	**WY**	P	*AN*	NL	52347	57347

CLASS 156 SUPER SPRINTER METRO-CAMMELL

DMSL–DMS.

Construction: Steel.
Engines: One Cummins NT855R5 of 213 kW (285 h.p.) at 2100 r.p.m.
Bogies: One P3-10 (powered) and one BT38 (non-powered).
Couplers: BSI.
Seating Layout: 2+2 facing/unidirectional.
Dimensions: 23.03 x 2.73 m.
Gangways: Throughout.   **Wheel Arrangement:** 2-B – B-2.
Doors: Single-leaf sliding.   **Maximum Speed:** 75 m.p.h.
Multiple Working: Within class and with Classes 142, 143, 144, 150, 153, 155, 158, 159, 170.

DMSL. Lot No. 31028 1988–1989. –/74 (†* –/72, st –/70, u –/68) 1TD 1W. 36.1 t.
DMS. Lot No. 31029 1987–1989. –/76 (q –/78, † –/74, tu –/72) 35.5 t.

Notes: 156 500–156 514 are owned by Strathclyde PTE, although managed by Angel.
Central Trains and First North Western units have been fitted with Chapman seating.
Arriva Trains Northern units have been fitted with Richmond seating.

Non standard livery: 156 429, 156 455 and 156 459 – All over dark blue with white doors.

156 401	r*	**CT**	P	*CT*	TS	52401	57401
156 402	r*	**P**	P	*CT*	TS	52402	57402
156 403	r*	**CT**	P	*CT*	TS	52403	57403
156 404	r*	**CT**	P	*CT*	TS	52404	57404
156 405	r*	**CT**	P	*CT*	TS	52405	57405
156 406	r*	**CT**	P	*CT*	TS	52406	57406
156 407	r*	**CT**	P	*CT*	TS	52407	57407
156 408	r*	**CT**	P	*CT*	TS	52408	57408
156 409	r*	**RE**	P	*CT*	TS	52409	57409
156 410	r*	**CT**	P	*CT*	TS	52410	57410
156 411	r*	**CT**	P	*CT*	TS	52411	57411
156 412	r*	**CT**	P	*CT*	TS	52412	57412
156 413	r*	**CT**	P	*CT*	TS	52413	57413
156 414	r*	**CT**	P	*CT*	TS	52414	57414
156 415	r*	**CT**	P	*CT*	TS	52415	57415

156 416	r*	RE	P	CT	TS	52416	57416	
156 417	r*	RE	P	CT	TS	52417	57417	
156 418	r*	RE	P	CT	TS	52418	57418	
156 419	r*	RE	P	CT	TS	52419	57419	
156 420	s	FS	P	NW	NH	52420	57420	LA' AL RATTY Ravenglass & Eskdale Railway
156 421	s	FS	P	NW	NH	52421	57421	
156 422	r*	RE	P	CT	TS	52422	57422	
156 423	s	FS	P	NW	NH	52423	57423	
156 424	s	FS	P	NW	NH	52424	57424	
156 425	s	RN	P	NW	NH	52425	57425	
156 426	s	RN	P	NW	NH	52426	57426	
156 427	s	FS	P	NW	NH	52427	57427	
156 428	s	FS	P	NW	NH	52428	57428	
156 429	s	0	P	NW	NH	52429	57429	
156 430	t	SC	A	SR	CK	52430	57430	
156 431	t	SC	A	SR	CK	52431	57431	
156 432	t	SC	A	SR	CK	52432	57432	
156 433	t	SC	A	SR	CK	52433	57433	The Kilmarnock Edition
156 434	t	SC	A	SR	CK	52434	57434	
156 435	t	SC	A	SR	CK	52435	57435	
156 436	†	SC	A	SR	CK	52436	57436	
156 437	t	SC	A	SR	CK	52437	57437	
156 438	q	NS	A	AN	NL	52438	57438	
156 439	t	SC	A	SR	CK	52439	57439	
156 440	s	FS	P	NW	NH	52440	57440	
156 441	s	FS	P	NW	NH	52441	57441	
156 442	t	SC	A	SR	CK	52442	57442	
156 443	q	NS	A	AN	HT	52443	57443	
156 444	q	NS	A	AN	HT	52444	57444	
156 445	u	SC	A	SR	CK	52445	57445	
156 446	t	FS	A	SR	CK	52446	57446	
156 447	ru	SR	A	SR	CK	52447	57447	
156 448	q	NS	A	AN	HT	52448	57448	
156 449	ru	SR	A	SR	CK	52449	57449	
156 450	rt	SR	A	SR	CK	52450	57450	
156 451	q	NS	A	AN	HT	52451	57451	
156 452	s	FS	P	NW	NH	52452	57452	
156 453	ru	SR	A	SR	CK	52453	57453	
156 454	q	NS	A	AN	HT	52454	57454	
156 455	s	0	P	NW	NH	52455	57455	
156 456	t	SR	A	SR	CK	52456	57456	
156 457	rt	SR	A	SR	CK	52457	57457	
156 458	rt	SR	A	SR	CK	52458	57458	
156 459	s	0	P	NW	NH	52459	57459	
156 460	s	RN	P	NW	NH	52460	57460	
156 461	s	RN	P	NW	NH	52461	57461	
156 462		SR	A	SR	CK	52462	57462	
156 463	q	NS	A	AN	HT	52463	57463	
156 464	s	RN	P	NW	NH	52464	57464	
156 465	ru	SR	A	SR	CK	52465	57465	

156 466	s	FS	P	NW	NH	52466	57466	BUXTON Festival
156 467		SR	A	SR	CK	52467	57467	
156 468	q	NS	A	AN	NL	52468	57468	
156 469	q	NS	A	AN	HT	52469	57469	
156 470	q	NS	A	AN	NL	52470	57470	
156 471	q	NS	A	AN	NL	52471	57471	
156 472	q	NS	A	AN	NL	52472	57472	
156 473	q	NS	A	AN	NL	52473	57473	
156 474	rt	SR	A	SR	CK	52474	57474	
156 475	q	NS	A	AN	NL	52475	57475	
156 476	rt	SR	A	SR	CK	52476	57476	
156 477	t	SR	A	SR	CK	52477	57477	
156 478	rt	SR	A	SR	CK	52478	57478	
156 479	q	NS	A	AN	NL	52479	57479	
156 480	q	NS	A	AN	NL	52480	57480	
156 481	q	NS	A	AN	NL	52481	57481	
156 482	q	NS	A	AN	NL	52482	57482	
156 483	q	NS	A	AN	NL	52483	57483	
156 484	q	NS	A	AN	NL	52484	57484	
156 485	ru	SR	A	SR	CK	52485	57485	
156 486	q	NS	A	AN	NL	52486	57486	
156 487	q	NS	A	AN	NL	52487	57487	
156 488	q	NS	A	AN	NL	52488	57488	
156 489	q	NS	A	AN	NL	52489	57489	
156 490	q	NS	A	AN	NL	52490	57490	
156 491	q	NS	A	AN	NL	52491	57491	
156 492	rt	SR	A	SR	CK	52492	57492	
156 493	rt	SR	A	SR	CK	52493	57493	
156 494	§	SC	A	SR	CK	52494	57494	
156 495	u	SC	A	SR	CK	52495	57495	
156 496	ru	SR	A	SR	CK	52496	57496	
156 497	q	NS	A	AN	NL	52497	57497	
156 498	q	NS	A	AN	NL	52498	57498	
156 499	rt	SR	A	SR	CK	52499	57499	
156 500	u	SC	A	SR	CK	52500	57500	
156 501		SC	A	SR	CK	52501	57501	
156 502		SC	A	SR	CK	52502	57502	
156 503		SC	A	SR	CK	52503	57503	
156 504		SC	A	SR	CK	52504	57504	
156 505		SC	A	SR	CK	52505	57505	
156 506		SC	A	SR	CK	52506	57506	
156 507		SC	A	SR	CK	52507	57507	
156 508		SC	A	SR	CK	52508	57508	
156 509		SC	A	SR	CK	52509	57509	
156 510		SC	A	SR	CK	52510	57510	
156 511		SC	A	SR	CK	52511	57511	
156 512		SC	A	SR	CK	52512	57512	
156 513		SC	A	SR	CK	52513	57513	
156 514		SC	A	SR	CK	52514	57514	

CLASS 158/0   BREL

DMSL(B)–DMSL(A) or DMCL–DMSL or DMCL–MSL–DMSL.

Construction: Welded aluminium.
Engines: 158 701–158 814: One Cummins NTA855R of 260 kW (350 h.p.) at 1900 r.p.m.
158 863–158 872: One Cummins NTA855R of 300 kW (400 h.p.) at 2100 r.p.m.
158 815–158 862: One Perkins 2006-TWH of 260 kW (350 h.p.) at 1900 r.p.m.
Bogies: One BREL P4 (powered) and one BREL T4 (non-powered) per car.
Couplers: BSI.
Seating Layout: 2+2 facing/unidirectional in all standard and first class unless
stated. 2+1 facing/unidirectional in 158 747–158 751 first class (declassified in
Wessex Trains units).
Dimensions: 22.57 x 2.70 m.
Gangways: Throughout.   **Wheel Arrangement:** 2-B – B-2.
Doors: Twin-leaf swing plug.   **Maximum Speed:** 90 m.p.h.
Multiple Working: Within class and with Classes 142, 143, 144, 150, 153, 155,
156, 159, 170.

DMSL(B). Lot No. 31051 BREL Derby 1989–1992. –/68 1TD 1W. († –/66 1TD 1W,
t –/64 1TD 1W). Public telephone and trolley space. 38.5 t.
MSL. Lot No. 31050 BREL Derby 1991. 37.1 t. –/70 2T. 37.1 t.
DMSL(A). Lot No. 31052 BREL Derby 1989–1992. –/70 1T († –/68 1T, t –/66 1T).
37.8 t.

The above details refer to the "as built" condition. The following DMSL(B) have
now been converted to DMCL as follows:

52701–52744 (First ScotRail/Trans-Pennine Express). 15/51 1TD 1W (* 15/53
1TD 1W).
52747–52751. (Wessex Trains/Trans-Pennine Express). 9/51 1TD 1W.
52760–52779/52781. (Trans-Pennine Express 2-car Units). 16/48 1TD 1W.
52798–52814 (Trans-Pennine Express 3-car Units). 32/32 1TD 1W.

s – Trans-Pennine and Central Trains units have been refurbished with new shape
seat cushions.
Trans-Pennine units are also fitted with table lamps in first class.
t – Arriva Trains Wales "Cambrian Line" units with some seats removed for
additional luggage space. Central Trains style seats (code s) retained.
† – Wessex Trains and Arriva Trains Wales units fitted with Chapman seating.

All First ScotRail 158s are "fitted" for RETB. When a unit arrives at Inverness the
cab display unit is clipped on and plugged in.

Non-standard livery: 158 750 – As **RE** but with a Trans-Pennine Express blue
band along the lower bodyside.

Advertising livery: 158 842 – Western Daily Mail (Silver, white and red with
various images).

158 701	*	**SR**	P	*SR*	IS	52701	57701	
158 702	*	**SR**	P	*SR*	IS	52702	57702	BBC Scotland – 75 Years
158 703	*	**SR**	P	*SR*	IS	52703	57703	
158 704	*	**SR**	P	*SR*	IS	52704	57704	

158 705	*	**SR**	P	*SR*	IS	52705	57705	
158 706	*	**SR**	P	*SR*	IS	52706	57706	
158 707	*	**SR**	P	*SR*	IS	52707	57707	Far North Line 125th ANNIVERSARY
158 708	*	**SR**	P	*SR*	IS	52708	57708	
158 709	*	**SR**	P	*SR*	IS	52709	57709	
158 710	*	**SR**	P	*SR*	IS	52710	57710	
158 711	*	**SR**	P	*SR*	IS	52711	57711	
158 712	*	**SR**	P	*SR*	IS	52712	57712	
158 713	*	**SR**	P	*SR*	IS	52713	57713	
158 714	*	**SR**	P	*SR*	IS	52714	57714	
158 715	*	**SR**	P	*SR*	IS	52715	57715	Haymarket
158 716	*	**SR**	P	*SR*	IS	52716	57716	
158 717	*	**SR**	P	*SR*	IS	52717	57717	
158 718	*	**SR**	P	*SR*	IS	52718	57718	
158 719	*	**SR**	P	*SR*	IS	52719	57719	
158 720	*	**SR**	P	*SR*	IS	52720	57720	
158 721	*	**SR**	P	*SR*	HA	52721	57721	
158 722	*	**SR**	P	*SR*	HA	52722	57722	
158 723	*	**SR**	P	*SR*	HA	52723	57723	
158 724	*	**SR**	P	*SR*	HA	52724	57724	
158 725	*	**SR**	P	*SR*	HA	52725	57725	
158 726	*	**SR**	P	*SR*	HA	52726	57726	
158 727	*	**SR**	P	*SR*	HA	52727	57727	
158 728	*	**SR**	P	*SR*	HA	52728	57728	
158 729	*	**SR**	P	*SR*	HA	52729	57729	
158 730	*	**SR**	P	*SR*	HA	52730	57730	
158 731	*	**SR**	P	*SR*	HA	52731	57731	
158 732	*	**SR**	P	*SR*	HA	52732	57732	
158 733	*	**SR**	P	*SR*	HA	52733	57733	
158 734	*	**SR**	P	*SR*	HA	52734	57734	
158 735	*	**SR**	P	*SR*	HA	52735	57735	
158 736	*	**SR**	P	*SR*	HA	52736	57736	
158 737		**TP**	P	*TP*	NL	52737	57737	
158 738	*	**SR**	P	*SR*	HA	52738	57738	
158 739	*	**SR**	P	*SR*	HA	52739	57739	
158 740	*	**SR**	P	*SR*	HA	52740	57740	
158 741	*	**SR**	P	*SR*	HA	52741	57741	
158 742		**TP**	P	*TP*	NL	52742	57742	
158 743		**TP**	P	*TP*	NL	52743	57743	
158 744		**TP**	P	*TP*	NL	52744	57744	
158 745	†	**WT**	P	*WX*	EX	52745	57745	
158 746	†	**WT**	P	*WX*	EX	52746	57746	
158 747		**WE**	P	*WX*	EX	52747	57747	
158 748		**WT**	P	*WX*	EX	52748	57748	
158 749		**WT**	P	*WX*	EX	52749	57749	
158 750		**0**	P	*TP*	NL	52750	57750	
158 751		**RE**	P	*WX*	EX	52751	57751	
158 752		**NW**	P	*NW*	NH	52752	57752	
158 753		**NW**	P	*NW*	NH	52753	57753	
158 754		**NW**	P	*NW*	NH	52754	57754	

158 755		**NW**	P	*NW*	NH	52755	57755	
158 756		**NW**	P	*NW*	NH	52756	57756	
158 757		**NW**	P	*TP*	NL	52757	57757	
158 758		**NW**	P	*TP*	NL	52758	57758	
158 759		**NW**	P	*NW*	NH	52759	57759	
158 760	s	**TP**	P	*TP*	NL	52760	57760	
158 761	s	**TP**	P	*TP*	NL	52761	57761	
158 762	s	**TP**	P	*TP*	NL	52762	57762	
158 763	s	**TP**	P	*TP*	NL	52763	57763	
158 764	s	**TP**	P	*TP*	NL	52764	57764	
158 765	s	**TP**	P	*TP*	NL	52765	57765	
158 766	s	**TP**	P	*TP*	NL	52766	57766	
158 767	s	**TP**	P	*TP*	NL	52767	57767	
158 768	s	**TP**	P	*TP*	NL	52768	57768	
158 769	s	**TP**	P	*TP*	NL	52769	57769	
158 770	s	**TP**	P	*TP*	NL	52770	57770	
158 771	s	**TP**	P	*TP*	HT	52771	57771	
158 772	s	**TP**	P	*TP*	HT	52772	57772	
158 773	s	**TP**	P	*TP*	HT	52773	57773	
158 774	s	**TP**	P	*TP*	NL	52774	57774	
158 775	s	**TP**	P	*TP*	HT	52775	57775	
158 776	s	**TP**	P	*TP*	HT	52776	57776	
158 777	s	**TP**	P	*TP*	HT	52777	57777	
158 778	s	**TP**	P	*TP*	HT	52778	57778	
158 779	s	**TP**	P	*TP*	HT	52779	57779	
158 780	s	**CT**	A	*CT*	TS	52780	57780	
158 781	s	**TP**	P	*TP*	HT	52781	57781	
158 782	s	**CT**	A	*WX*	EX	52782	57782	
158 783	s	**CT**	A	*CT*	TS	52783	57783	
158 784	s	**CT**	A	*CT*	TS	52784	57784	
158 785	s	**CT**	A	*CT*	TS	52785	57785	
158 786	s	**CT**	A	*CT*	TS	52786	57786	
158 787	s	**CT**	A	*CT*	TS	52787	57787	
158 788	s	**CT**	A	*CT*	TS	52788	57788	
158 789	s	**CT**	A	*CT*	TS	52789	57789	
158 790	s	**CT**	A	*CT*	TS	52790	57790	
158 791	s	**CT**	A	*CT*	TS	52791	57791	
158 792	s	**CT**	A	*CT*	TS	52792	57792	
158 793	s	**CT**	A	*CT*	TS	52793	57793	
158 794	s	**CT**	A	*CT*	TS	52794	57794	
158 795	s	**CT**	A	*CT*	TS	52795	57795	
158 796	s	**CT**	A	*CT*	TS	52796	57796	
158 797	s	**CT**	A	*CT*	TS	52797	57797	
158 798	s	**TP**	P	*TP*	HT	52798	58715	57798
158 799	s	**TP**	P	*TP*	HT	52799	58716	57799
158 800	s	**TP**	P	*TP*	HT	52800	58717	57800
158 801	s	**TP**	P	*TP*	HT	52801	58701	57801
158 802	s	**TP**	P	*TP*	HT	52802	58702	57802
158 803	s	**TP**	P	*TP*	HT	52803	58703	57803
158 804	s	**TP**	P	*TP*	HT	52804	58704	57804
158 805	s	**TP**	P	*TP*	HT	52805	58705	57805

158 806	s	**TP**	P	*TP*	HT	52806	58706	57806
158 807	s	**TP**	P	*TP*	HT	52807	58707	57807
158 808	s	**TP**	P	*TP*	HT	52808	58708	57808
158 809	s	**TP**	P	*TP*	HT	52809	58709	57809
158 810	s	**TP**	P	*TP*	HT	52810	58710	57810
158 811	s	**TP**	P	*TP*	HT	52811	58711	57811
158 812	s	**TP**	P	*TP*	HT	52812	58712	57812
158 813	s	**TP**	P	*TP*	HT	52813	58713	57813
158 814	s	**TP**	P	*TP*	HT	52814	58714	57814
158 815	†	**WT**	A	*WX*	EX	52815	57815	
158 816	†	**WT**	A	*WX*	EX	52816	57816	
158 817	†	**WB**	A	*WX*	EX	52817	57817	
158 818	†	**AV**	A	*AW*	CF	52818	57818	
158 819	†	**GP**	A	*AW*	CF	52819	57819	
158 820	†	**AV**	A	*AW*	CF	52820	57820	
158 821	†	**GP**	A	*AW*	CF	52821	57821	
158 822	†	**WB**	A	*AW*	CF	52822	57822	
158 823	†	**WB**	A	*AW*	CF	52823	57823	
158 824	†	**WB**	A	*AW*	CF	52824	57824	
158 825	†	**GP**	A	*AW*	CF	52825	57825	
158 826	†	**WB**	A	*AW*	CF	52826	57826	
158 827	†	**GP**	A	*AW*	CF	52827	57827	
158 828	†	**AV**	A	*AW*	CF	52828	57828	
158 829	†	**WB**	A	*AW*	CF	52829	57829	
158 830	†	**WB**	A	*AW*	CF	52830	57830	
158 831	†	**WB**	A	*AW*	CF	52831	57831	
158 832	†	**WB**	A	*AW*	CF	52832	57832	
158 833	†	**WB**	A	*AW*	CF	52833	57833	
158 834	†	**WB**	A	*AW*	CF	52834	57834	
158 835	†	**WB**	A	*AW*	CF	52835	57835	
158 836	†	**WB**	A	*AW*	CF	52836	57836	
158 837	†	**RE**	A	*AW*	CF	52837	57837	
158 838	†	**WB**	A	*AW*	CF	52838	57838	
158 839	†	**WB**	A	*AW*	CF	52839	57839	
158 840	†	**RE**	A	*AW*	CF	52840	57840	
158 841	†	**GP**	A	*AW*	CF	52841	57841	
158 842	†	**AL**	A	*AW*	CF	52842	57842	
158 843	†	**WB**	A	*AW*	CF	52843	57843	
158 844	rt	**CT**	A	*AW*	CF	52844	57844	
158 845	rt	**CT**	A	*AW*	CF	52845	57845	
158 846	rt	**CT**	A	*AW*	CF	52846	57846	
158 847	rt	**CT**	A	*AW*	CF	52847	57847	
158 848	rt	**CT**	A	*AW*	CF	52848	57848	
158 849	rt	**CT**	A	*AW*	CF	52849	57849	
158 850	rt	**CT**	A	*AW*	CF	52850	57850	
158 851	rt	**CT**	A	*AW*	CF	52851	57851	
158 852	rt	**CT**	A	*AW*	CF	52852	57852	
158 853	rt	**CT**	A	*AW*	CF	52853	57853	
158 854	rt	**CT**	A	*AW*	CF	52854	57854	
158 855	s	**WE**	A	*WX*	EX	52855	57855	Exmoor Explorer
158 856	s	**CT**	A	*CT*	TS	52856	57856	

158 857	s	**CT**	A	*CT*	TS	52857 57857
158 858	s	**CT**	A	*CT*	TS	52858 57858
158 859	s	**CT**	A	*WX*	EX	52859 57859
158 860	s	**CT**	A	*CT*	TS	52860 57860
158 861	s	**CT**	A	*WX*	EX	52861 57861
158 862	s	**CT**	A	*CT*	TS	52862 57862
158 863	†	**WT**	A	*WX*	EX	52863 57863
158 864	†	**WT**	A	*WX*	EX	52864 57864
158 865	†	**WT**	A	*WX*	EX	52865 57865
158 866	†	**WT**	A	*WX*	EX	52866 57866
158 867	†	**WT**	A	*WX*	EX	52867 57867
158 868	†	**WT**	A	*WX*	EX	52868 57868
158 869	†	**WT**	A	*WX*	EX	52869 57869
158 870	†	**WT**	A	*WX*	EX	52870 57870
158 871	†	**WT**	A	*WX*	EX	52871 57871
158 872	†	**WT**	A	*WX*	EX	52872 57872

CLASS 158/9   BREL

DMSL–DMS. Units leased by West Yorkshire PTE. Details as for Class 158/0 except for seating layout and toilets.

DMSL. Lot No. 31051 BREL Derby 1990–1992. –/70 1TD 1W. Public telephone and trolley space. 38.1 t.
DMS. Lot No. 31052 BREL Derby 1990–1992. –/72 and parcels area. 37.8 t.

Note: These units are leased by West Yorkshire PTE and are managed by Porterbrook Leasing Company.

158 901	**YP**	P	*AN*	NL	52901 57901
158 902	**YP**	P	*AN*	NL	52902 57902
158 903	**YP**	P	*AN*	NL	52903 57903
158 904	**YP**	P	*AN*	NL	52904 57904
158 905	**YP**	P	*AN*	NL	52905 57905
158 906	**YP**	P	*AN*	NL	52906 57906
158 907	**YP**	P	*AN*	NL	52907 57907
158 908	**YP**	P	*AN*	NL	52908 57908
158 909	**YP**	P	*AN*	NL	52909 57909
158 910	**YP**	P	*AN*	NL	52910 57910

CLASS 159   BREL

DMCL–MSL–DMSL. Built as Class 158. Converted before entering passenger service to Class 159 by Rosyth Dockyard.

Construction: Welded aluminium.
Engines: One Cummins NTA855R of 300 kW (400 h.p.) at 2100 r.p.m.
Bogies: One BREL P4 (powered) and one BREL T4 (non-powered) per car.
Couplers: BSI.
Seating Layout: 1: 2+1 facing, 2: 2+2 facing/unidirectional.
Dimensions: 23.21 x 2.82 m.
Gangways: Throughout.   **Wheel Arrangement:** 2-B – B-2 – B-2.
Doors: Twin-leaf swing plug.   **Maximum Speed:** 90 m.p.h.
Multiple Working: Within class and with Classes 142, 143, 144, 150, 153, 155, 156, 158, 170.

DMCL. Lot No. 31051 BREL Derby 1992–1993. 24/28 1TD 1W. 38.5 t.
MSL. Lot No. 31050 BREL Derby 1992–1993. 38.0 t. –/72 1T and parcels area.
DMSL. Lot No. 31052 BREL Derby 1992–1993. –/72 1T and parcels area. 37.8 t.

Note: Vehicle 58718 is out of service with fire damage.

159 001	**SW** P	*SW*	SA	52873	58734	57873	CITY OF EXETER
159 002	**SW** P	*SW*	SA	52874	58719	57874	CITY OF SALISBURY
159 003	**SW** P	*SW*	SA	52875	58720	57875	TEMPLECOMBE
159 004	**SW** P	*SW*	SA	52876	58721	57876	BASINGSTOKE AND DEANE
159 005	**SW** P	*SW*	SA	52877	58722	57877	
159 006	**SW** P	*SW*	SA	52878	58723	57878	
159 007	**SW** P	*SW*	SA	52879	58724	57879	
159 008	**SW** P	*SW*	SA	52880	58725	57880	
159 009	**SW** P	*SW*	SA	52881	58726	57881	
159 010	**SW** P	*SW*	SA	52882	58727	57882	
159 011	**SW** P	*SW*	SA	52883	58728	57883	
159 012	**SW** P	*SW*	SA	52884	58729	57884	
159 013	**SW** P	*SW*	SA	52885	58730	57885	
159 014	**SW** P	*SW*	SA	52886	58731	57886	
159 015	**SW** P	*SW*	SA	52887	58732	57887	
159 016	**SW** P	*SW*	SA	52888	58733	57888	
159 017	**SW** P		SA	52889		57889	
159 018	**SW** P	*SW*	SA	52890	58735	57890	
159 019	**SW** P	*SW*	SA	52891	58736	57891	
159 020	**SW** P	*SW*	SA	52892	58737	57892	
159 021	**SW** P	*SW*	SA	52893	58738	57893	
159 022	**SW** P	*SW*	SA	52894	58739	57894	
Spare	**SW** P		ZC		58718		

CLASS 165/0   NETWORK TURBO   BREL

DMCL–DMS and DMCL–MS–DMS. Chiltern units had their first class seats declassified from January 2003. They are being refurbished and fitted with air-conditioning and DMCLs converted to DMSL.

Construction: Welded aluminium.
Engines: One Perkins 2006-TWH of 260 kW (350 h.p.) at 1900 r.p.m.
Bogies: BREL P3-17 (powered), BREL T3-17 (non-powered).
Couplers: BSI.
Seating Layout: 1: 2+2 facing. 2: Unrefurbished units: 3+2 facing/unidirectional. 2: Refurbished Chiltern units: 2+2/3+2 facing/unidirectional.
Dimensions: 23.50 x 2.85 m.
Gangways: Within unit only.   **Wheel Arrangement:** 2-B (– B-2) – B-2.
Doors: Twin-leaf swing plug.   **Maximum Speed:** 75 m.p.h.
Multiple Working: Within class and with Classes 166 and 168.

58801–58822 and 58873–58878. DMCL (as built). Lot No. 31087 BREL York 1990. 16/72 1T (* –/89 1T, † –/82 1T). 37.0 t.
58801–58822 and 58873–58878. DMSL (refurbished)*. Lot No. 31087 BREL York 1990. –/89 1T, († –/82 1T). 37.0 t.
58823–58833. DMSL. Lot No. 31089 BREL York 1991–1992. 24/60 1T (* –/89 1T). 37.0 t.
MS. Lot No. 31090 BREL York 1991–1992. –/106. 37.0 t.
DMS. Lot No. 31088 BREL York 1991–1992. –/98 (* –/94). 37.0 t.

Notes:

† Trial refurbished Chiltern Railways unit.
* Fully refurbished Chiltern Railways units.
165 001–165 039 are fitted with tripcocks for working over London Underground tracks between Harrow-on-the-Hill and Amersham.

165 001	*	CR	A	CR	AL	58801	58834
165 002		NT	A	FK	RG	58802	58835
165 003		TT	A	FK	RG	58803	58836
165 004	*	CR	A	CR	AL	58804	58837
165 005		TT	A	FK	RG	58805	58838
165 006		NT	A	CR	AL	58806	58839
165 007		NT	A	CR	AL	58807	58840
165 008	*	CR	A	CR	AL	58808	58841
165 009		NT	A	CR	AL	58809	58842
165 010		NT	A	CR	AL	58810	58843
165 011	*	CR	A	CR	AL	58811	58844
165 012		NT	A	CR	AL	58812	58845
165 013	†	CR	A	CR	AL	58813	58846
165 014		NT	A	CR	AL	58814	58847
165 015	*	CR	A	CR	AL	58815	58848
165 016	*	CR	A	CR	AL	58816	58849
165 017	*	CR	A	CR	AL	58817	58850
165 018	*	CR	A	CR	AL	58818	58851
165 019		NT	A	CR	AL	58819	58852

165 020	*	**CR**	A	*CR*	AL	58820		58853
165 021	*	**CR**	A	*CR*	AL	58821		58854
165 022		**NT**	A	*CR*	AL	58822		58855
165 023		**NT**	A	*CR*	AL	58873		58867
165 024	*	**CR**	A	*CR*	AL	58874		58868
165 025		**NT**	A	*CR*	AL	58875		58869
165 026	*	**CR**	A	*CR*	AL	58876		58870
165 027	*	**CR**	A	*CR*	AL	58877		58871
165 028	*	**CR**	A	*CR*	AL	58878		58872
165 029	*	**CR**	A	*CR*	AL	58823	55404	58856
165 030	*	**CR**	A	*CR*	AL	58824	55405	58857
165 031	*	**CR**	A	*CR*	AL	58825	55406	58858
165 032	*	**CR**	A	*CR*	AL	58826	55407	58859
165 033		**NT**	A	*CR*	AL	58827	55408	58860
165 034	*	**CR**	A	*CR*	AL	58828	55409	58861
165 035	*	**CR**	A	*CR*	AL	58829	55410	58862
165 036	*	**CR**	A	*CR*	AL	58830	55411	58863
165 037		**NT**	A	*CR*	AL	58831	55412	58864
165 038		**NT**	A	*CR*	AL	58832	55413	58865
165 039		**NT**	A	*CR*	AL	58833	55414	58866

CLASS 165/1   NETWORK TURBO   BREL

First Great Western Link units. DMCL–MS–DMS or DMCL–DMS.

Construction: Welded aluminium.
Engines: One Perkins 2006-TWH of 260 kW (350 h.p.) at 1900 r.p.m.
Bogies: BREL P3-17 (powered), BREL T3-17 (non-powered).
Couplers: BSI.
Seating Layout: 1: 2+2 facing, 2: 3+2 facing/unidirectional.
Dimensions: 23.50 x 2.85 m.
Gangways: Within unit only.   **Wheel Arrangement:** 2-B (– B-2) – B-2.
Doors: Twin-leaf swing plug.   **Maximum Speed:** 90 m.p.h.
Multiple Working: Within class and with Classes 166 and 168.

58953–58969. DMCL. Lot No. 31098 BREL York 1992. 16/66 1T. 37.0 t.
58879–58898. DMCL. Lot No. 31096 BREL York 1992. 16/72 1T. 37.0 t.
MS. Lot No. 31099 BREL 1992. –/106. 37.0 t.
DMS. Lot No. 31097 BREL 1992. –/98. 37.0 t.

165 101	**TT**	A	*FK*	RG	58953	55415	58916
165 102	**TT**	A	*FK*	RG	58954	55416	58917
165 103	**TT**	A	*FK*	RG	58955	55417	58918
165 104	**TT**	A	*FK*	RG	58956	55418	58919
165 105	**TT**	A	*FK*	RG	58957	55419	58920
165 106	**TT**	A	*FK*	RG	58958	55420	58921
165 107	**TT**	A	*FK*	RG	58959	55421	58922
165 108	**TT**	A	*FK*	RG	58960	55422	58923

165 109	TT	A	FK	RG	58961	55423	58924
165 110	TT	A	FK	RG	58962	55424	58925
165 111	TT	A	FK	RG	58963	55425	58926
165 112	TT	A	FK	RG	58964	55426	58927
165 113	TT	A	FK	RG	58965	55427	58928
165 114	TT	A	FK	RG	58966	55428	58929
165 116	TT	A	FK	RG	58968	55430	58931
165 117	TT	A	FK	RG	58969	55431	58932
165 118	TT	A	FK	RG	58879		58933
165 119	TT	A	FK	RG	58880		58934
165 120	TT	A	FK	RG	58881		58935
165 121	TT	A	FK	RG	58882		58936
165 122	TT	A	FK	RG	58883		58937
165 123	TT	A	FK	RG	58884		58938
165 124	TT	A	FK	RG	58885		58939
165 125	TT	A	FK	RG	58886		58940
165 126	TT	A	FK	RG	58887		58941
165 127	TT	A	FK	RG	58888		58942
165 128	TT	A	FK	RG	58889		58943
165 129	TT	A	FK	RG	58890		58944
165 130	TT	A	FK	RG	58891		58945
165 131	TT	A	FK	RG	58892		58946
165 132	TT	A	FK	RG	58893		58947
165 133	TT	A	FK	RG	58894		58948
165 134	TT	A	FK	RG	58895		58949
165 135	TT	A	FK	RG	58896		58950
165 136	TT	A	FK	RG	58897		58951
165 137	TT	A	FK	RG	58898		58952

CLASS 166   NETWORK EXPRESS TURBO   ABB

DMCL(A)–MS–DMCL(B). First Great Western Link units, built for Paddington–Oxford/Newbury services. Air Conditioned.

Construction: Welded aluminium.
Engines: One Perkins 2006-TWH of 260 kW (350 h.p.) at 1900 r.p.m.
Bogies: BREL P3-17 (powered), BREL T3-17 (non-powered).
Couplers: BSI.
Seating Layout: 1: 2+2 facing, 2: 3+2 facing/unidirectional. 20 standard class seats in 2+2 format in DMCL(B).
Dimensions: 23.50 x 2.85 m.
Gangways: Within unit only.   **Wheel Arrangement:** 2-B – B-2 – B-2.
Doors: Twin-leaf swing plug.   **Maximum Speed:** 90 m.p.h.
Multiple Working: Within class and with Classes 165 and 168.

DMCL (A). Lot No. 31116 ABB York 1992–1993. 16/75 1T. 40.62 t.
MS. Lot No. 31117 ABB York 1992–1993. –/96. 38.04 t.
DMCL (B). Lot No. 31116 ABB York 1992–1993. 16/72 1T. 40.64 t.

166 201	TT	A	FK	RG	58101	58601	58122
166 202	TT	A	FK	RG	58102	58602	58123
166 203	TT	A	FK	RG	58103	58603	58124
166 204	TT	A	FK	RG	58104	58604	58125
166 205	TT	A	FK	RG	58105	58605	58126
166 206	TT	A	FK	RG	58106	58606	58127
166 207	TT	A	FK	RG	58107	58607	58128
166 208	TT	A	FK	RG	58108	58608	58129
166 209	TT	A	FK	RG	58109	58609	58130
166 210	TT	A	FK	RG	58110	58610	58131
166 211	TT	A	FK	RG	58111	58611	58132
166 212	TT	A	FK	RG	58112	58612	58133
166 213	TT	A	FK	RG	58113	58613	58134
166 214	TT	A	FK	RG	58114	58614	58135
166 215	TT	A	FK	RG	58115	58615	58136
166 216	TT	A	FK	RG	58116	58616	58137
166 217	TT	A	FK	RG	58117	58617	58138
166 218	TT	A	FK	RG	58118	58618	58139
166 219	TT	A	FK	RG	58119	58619	58140
166 220	TT	A	FK	RG	58120	58620	58141
166 221	TT	A	FK	RG	58121	58621	58142

CLASS 168 CLUBMAN ADTRANZ/BOMBARDIER

Various formations. Air conditioned.

Construction: Welded aluminium bodies with bolt-on steel ends.
Engines: One MTU 6R183TD13H of 315 kW (422 h.p.) at 1900 r.p.m.
Transmission: Hydraulic. Voith T211rzze to ZF final drive.
Bogies: One Adtranz P3–23 and one BREL T3–23 per car.
Couplers: BSI.
Seating Layout: 2+2 facing/unidirectional.
Dimensions: 23.62 x 2.69 m.
Gangways: Within unit only.   **Wheel Arrangement:** 2-B (– B-2 – B-2) – B-2.
Doors: Twin-leaf swing plug.   **Maximum Speed:** 100 m.p.h.
Multiple Working: Within class and with Classes 165 and 166.

Fitted with tripcocks for working over London Underground tracks between Harrow-on-the-Hill and Amersham.

Class 168/0. Original Design. DMSL(A)–MSL–MS–DMSL(B).

58151–58155. DMSL(A). Adtranz Derby 1997–1998. –/60 1TD 1W. 43.7 t.
58651–58655. MSL. Adtranz Derby 1998. –/73 1T. 41.0 t.
58451–58455. MS. Adtranz Derby 1998. –/77. 40.5 t.
58251–58255. DMSL(B). Adtranz Derby 1998. –/68 1T. 43.6 t.

Note: 58451–58455 were formerly numbered 58656–58660 in 168 106–168 110.

168 001	CR	P	CR	AL	58151	58651	58451	58251
168 002	CR	P	CR	AL	58152	58652	58452	58252
168 003	CR	P	CR	AL	58153	58653	58453	58253
168 004	CR	P	CR	AL	58154	58654	58454	58254
168 005	CR	P	CR	AL	58155	58655	58455	58255

Class 168/1. These units are effectively Class 170s. DMSL(A)–(MS)–MSL–DMSL(B).

58156–58163. DMSL(A). Adtranz Derby 2000. –/59 1TD 2W. 43.7 t.
58756–58757. MSL. Bombardier Derby 2002. –/73 1T. 41.0 t.
58456–58460. MS. Bombardier Derby 2002. –/76. 40.5 t.
58461–58463. MS. Adtranz Derby 2000. –/76. 42.4 t.
58256–58263. DMSL(B). Adtranz Derby 2000. –/69 1T. 43.6 t.

Note: 58461–58463 have been renumbered from 58661–58663.

168 106	**CR**	P	*CR*	AL	58156	58456	58756	58256
168 107	**CR**	P	*CR*	AL	58157	58457	58757	58257
168 108	**CR**	P	*CR*	AL	58158	58458		58258
168 109	**CR**	P	*CR*	AL	58159	58459		58259
168 110	**CR**	P	*CR*	AL	58160	58460		58260
168 111	**CR**	H	*CR*	AL	58161	58461		58261
168 112	**CR**	H	*CR*	AL	58162	58462		58262
168 113	**CR**	H	*CR*	AL	58163	58463		58263

Class 168/2. These units are effectively Class 170s. DMSL–(MS)–DMSL.

58164–58169. DMSL(A). Bombardier Derby 2003–2004. –/59 1TD 2W. 45.4 t.
58464/58468/58469. MS. Bombardier Derby 2003–2004. –/76. 44.0 t.
58264–58269. DMSL(B). Bombardier Derby 2003–2004. –/69 1T. 45.4 t.

168 214	**CR**	P	*CR*	AL	58164	58464	58264
168 215	**CR**	P	*CR*	AL	58165		58265
168 216	**CR**	P	*CR*	AL	58166		58266
168 217	**CR**	P	*CR*	AL	58167		58267
168 218	**CR**	P	*CR*	AL	58168	58468	58268
168 219	**CR**	P	*CR*	AL	58169	58469	58269

CLASS 170 TURBOSTAR ADTRANZ/BOMBARDIER

Various formations. Air conditioned.

Construction: Welded aluminium bodies with bolt-on steel ends.
Engines: One MTU 6R183TD13H of 315 kW (422 h.p.) at 1900 r.p.m.
Transmission: Hydraulic. Voith T211rzze to ZF final drive.
Bogies: One Adtranz P3–23 and one BREL T3–23 per car.
Couplers: BSI.
Seating Layout: 1: 2+1 facing/unidirectional (2+2 in first class in Class 170/1 end cars). 2: 2+2 facing/unidirectional.
Dimensions: 23.62 x 2.69 m.
Gangways: Within unit only.   **Wheel Arrangement:** 2-B (– B-2) – B-2.
Doors: Twin-leaf swing plug.   **Maximum Speed:** 100 m.p.h.
Multiple Working: Within class and with classes 150, 153, 155, 156, 158 and 159.

Class 170/1. Units built for Midland Mainline. DMCL–MCRMB–DMCL or DMCL–DMCL. All due to be transferred to Central Trains by the end of January 2005.

DMCL (A). Adtranz Derby 1998–1999. 12/45 1TD 2W. 45.19 t.
MCRMB. Adtranz Derby 2001. 21/22 and bar. 43.00 t.
DMCL (B). Adtranz Derby 1998–1999. 12/52 1T. Catering point. 45.22 t

Note: The DMCL(A) and DMCL(B) in the 3-car units have had their former first class end sections declassified.

170 101	**MM**	P	*CT*	TS	50101	55101	79101
170 102	**MM**	P	*CT*	TS	50102	55102	79102
170 103	**MM**	P	*CT*	TS	50103	55103	79103
170 104	**MM**	P	*CT*	TS	50104	55104	79104
170 105	**MM**	P	*CT*	TS	50105	55105	79105
170 106	**MM**	P	*CT*	TS	50106	55106	79106
170 107	**MM**	P	*CT*	TS	50107	55107	79107
170 108	**MM**	P	*CT*	TS	50108	55108	79108
170 109	**MM**	P	*CT*	TS	50109	55109	79109
170 110	**MM**	P	*CT*	TS	50110	55110	79110
170 111	**MM**	P	*MM*	DY	50111		79111
170 112	**MM**	P	*MM*	DY	50112		79112
170 113	**MM**	P	*MM*	DY	50113		79113
170 114	**MM**	P	*MM*	DY	50114		79114
170 115	**MM**	P	*MM*	DY	50115		79115
170 116	**MM**	P	*CT*	TS	50116		79116
170 117	**MM**	P	*CT*	TS	50117		79117

Class 170/2. One Anglia 3-car units. DMCL–MSLRB–DMSL.

DMCL. Adtranz Derby 1999. 29/3 1TD 2W. 44.30 t.
MSLRB. Adtranz Derby 1999. –/58 1T. Buffet and guard's office. 42.76 t.
DMSL. Adtranz Derby 1999. –/66 1T. 44.70 t.

170 201	**AN**	P	*1A*	NC	50201	56201	79201
170 202	**1**	P	*1A*	NC	50202	56202	79202
170 203	**1**	P	*1A*	NC	50203	56203	79203

170 204	**AN**	P	*1A*	NC	50204	56204	79204
170 205	**AN**	P	*1A*	NC	50205	56205	79205
170 206	**AN**	P	*1A*	NC	50206	56206	79206
170 207	**1**	P	*1A*	NC	50207	56207	79207
170 208	**1**	P	*1A*	NC	50208	56208	79208

Class 170/2. One Anglia 2-car units. DMSL–DMCL.

DMSL. Bombardier Derby 2002. –/57 1TD 2W. 44.30 t.
DMCL. Bombardier Derby 2002. 9/53 1T. 44.70 t.

170 270	**1**	P	*1A*	NC	50270	79270
170 271	**AN**	P	*1A*	NC	50271	79271
170 272	**AN**	P	*1A*	NC	50272	79272
170 273	**AN**	P	*1A*	NC	50273	79273

Class 170/3. South West Trains units. DMCL–DMCL or DMCL–DMSL.

50301–50308. DMCL(A). Adtranz Derby 2000. 9/43 1TD 2W. 45.80 t.
50392. DMCL(A). Bombardier Derby 2003. 9/43 1TD 2W. . t.
79301–79308. DMCL(B). Adtranz Derby 2000. 9/53 1T. 45.80 t.
79392. DMCL(B). Bombardier Derby 2003. 9/53 1T. . t.

Note: 170 392 was initially numbered 170 727 in error and painted into Southern livery before being repainted into South West Trains livery.

170 301	**SW**	P	*SW*	SA	50301	79301
170 302	**SW**	P	*SW*	SA	50302	79302
170 303	**SW**	P	*SW*	SA	50303	79303
170 304	**SW**	P	*SW*	SA	50304	79304
170 305	**SW**	P	*SW*	SA	50305	79305
170 306	**SW**	P	*SW*	SA	50306	79306
170 307	**SW**	P	*SW*	SA	50307	79307
170 308	**SW**	P	*SW*	SA	50308	79308
170 392	**SW**	P	*SW*	SA	50392	79392

Class 170/3. Hull Trains units. DMCL–MSLRB–DMSL.

DMCL. Bombardier Derby 2004. 29/5 1TD 2W. 44.30 t.
MSLRB. Bombardier Derby 2004. –/60 1T. Buffet and guard's office 42.76 t.
DMSL. Bombardier Derby 2004. –/71 1T. 47.0 t.

170 393	**HT**	P	*HT*	IL	50393	56393	79393
170 394	**HT**	P	*HT*	IL	50394	56394	79394
170 395	**HT**	P	*HT*	IL	50395	56395	79395
170 396	**HT**	P	*HT*	IL	50396	56396	79396

Class 170/3. Porterbrook spot hire units. DMCL–MC–DMCL.

DMCL(A). Bombardier Derby 2002. 9/43 1TD 1W. 45.40 t.
MC. Bombardier Derby 2002. 22/36. 41.60 t.
DMCL(B). Bombardier Derby 2002. 9/53 1T. 45.80 t.

| 170 397 | **P** | P | *CT* | TS | 50397 | 56397 | 79397 |
| 170 398 | **P** | P | *CT* | TS | 50398 | 56398 | 79398 |

Class 170/3. Porterbrook spot hire unit. DMCL–DMCL.

DMCL(A). Bombardier Derby 2001. 9/43 1TD 2W. 45.40 t.
DMCL(B). Bombardier Derby 2001. 9/53 1T. 45.80 t.

Advertising Livery: 170 399 Derwent Valley Mills World Heritage Site (green, grey and blue with various images).

170 399	**AL**	P	*CT*	TS	50399	79399

Class 170/4. First ScotRail "express" units. DMCL–MS–DMCL.

DMCL(A). Adtranz Derby 1999–2001. 9/43 1TD 2W. 45.80 t.
MS. Adtranz Derby 1999–2001. –/76. 43.00 t.
DMCL(B). Adtranz Derby 1999–2001. 9/53 1T. 45.80 t.

170 401	**FS**	P	*SR*	HA	50401	56401	79401
170 402	**SR**	P	*SR*	HA	50402	56402	79402
170 403	**SR**	P	*SR*	HA	50403	56403	79403
170 404	**SR**	P	*SR*	HA	50404	56404	79404
170 405	**FS**	P	*SR*	HA	50405	56405	79405
170 406	**SR**	P	*SR*	HA	50406	56406	79406
170 407	**SR**	P	*SR*	HA	50407	56407	79407
170 408	**SR**	P	*SR*	HA	50408	56408	79408
170 409	**SR**	P	*SR*	HA	50409	56409	79409
170 410	**SR**	P	*SR*	HA	50410	56410	79410
170 411	**SR**	P	*SR*	HA	50411	56411	79411
170 412	**SR**	P	*SR*	HA	50412	56412	79412
170 413	**SR**	P	*SR*	HA	50413	56413	79413
170 414	**SR**	P	*SR*	HA	50414	56414	79414
170 415	**SR**	P	*SR*	HA	50415	56415	79415
170 416	**SR**	H	*SR*	HA	50416	56416	79416
170 417	**SR**	H	*SR*	HA	50417	56417	79417
170 418	**SR**	H	*SR*	HA	50418	56418	79418
170 419	**SR**	H	*SR*	HA	50419	56419	79419
170 420	**SR**	H	*SR*	HA	50420	56420	79420
170 421	**SR**	H	*SR*	HA	50421	56421	79421
170 422	**SR**	H	*SR*	HA	50422	56422	79422
170 423	**SR**	H	*SR*	HA	50423	56423	79423
170 424	**SR**	H	*SR*	HA	50424	56424	79424

Class 170/4. First ScotRail "express" units. DMCL–MS–DMSL or DMCL–MS–DMSL (see notes below).

DMCL. Bombardier Derby 2003–2005. 9/43 1TD 2W. 45.80 t.
MS. Bombardier Derby 2003–2005. –/76. 43.00 t.
DMSL. Bombardier Derby 2003–2005. –/67 1T. 45.80 t.

IMPORTANT NOTE: 170 425–170 432 were delivered DMCL–MS–DMSL, to become DMCL–MS–DMCL.
The DMSL/DMCLs of units 170 425–170 432 and 170 450–170 457 will be swapped when the latter units have been delivered.

170 425	**SR**	P	*SR*	HA	50425	56425	79450
170 426	**SR**	P	*SR*	HA	50426	56426	79451
170 427	**SR**	P	*SR*	HA	50427	56427	79452

170 428	**SR**	P	*SR*	HA	50428	56428	79453
170 429	**SR**	P	*SR*	HA	50429	56429	79454
170 430	**SR**	P	*SR*	HA	50430	56430	79455
170 431	**SR**	P	*SR*	HA	50431	56431	79456
170 432	**SR**	P	*SR*	HA	50432	56432	79457
170 433		P			50433	56433	79433
170 434		P			50434	56434	79434

Class 170/4. First ScotRail "suburban" units. On order. DMSL–MS–DMCL or DMSL–MS–DMSL (see notes below).

DMSL. Bombardier Derby 2004–2005. –/55 1TD 2W. 45.80 t.
MS. Bombardier Derby 2004–2005. –/76. 43.00 t.
DMCL. Bombardier Derby 2004–2005. 9/53 1T. 45.80 t.

IMPORTANT NOTE: 170 450–170 457 to be delivered DMSL–MS–DMCL, to become DMSL–MS–DMSL.

The DMCL/DMSLs of units 170 450–170 457 and 170 425–170 432 will be swapped as the suburban units are delivered.

170 450		P			50450	56450	79425
170 451		P			50451	56451	79426
170 452		P			50452	56452	79427
170 453		P			50453	56453	79428
170 454		P			50454	56454	79429
170 455		P			50455	56455	79430
170 456		P			50456	56456	79431
170 457		P			50457	56457	79432
170 458	**P**	P	*SR*	HA	50458	56458	79458
170 459	**P**	P	*SR*	HA	50459	56459	79459
170 460		P			50460	56460	79460
170 461		P			50461	56461	79461

Class 170/4. First ScotRail units. Standard class only Strathclyde PTE units. DMSL–MS–DMSL.

50470–50471. DMSL(A). Adtranz Derby 2001. –/55 1TD 2W. 45.80 t.
50472–50478. DMSL(A). Bombardier Derby 2004–2005. –/57 1TD 2W.   . t.
56470–56471. MS. Adtranz Derby 2001. –/76. 43.00 t.
56472–56478. MS. Bombardier Derby 2004–2005. –/76.   . t.
79470–79471. DMSL(B). Adtranz Derby 2001. –/67 1T. 45.80 t.
79472–79478. DMSL(B). Bombardier Derby 2004–2005. –/67 1T. 46.36 t.

170 470	**SC**	P	*SR*	HA	50470	56470	79470
170 471	**SC**	P	*SR*	HA	50471	56471	79471
170 472	**SP**	P	*SR*	HA	50472	56472	79472
170 473	**SP**	P	*SR*	HA	50473	56473	79473
170 474	**SP**	P	*SR*	HA	50474	56474	79474
170 475	**SP**	P	*SR*	HA	50475	56475	79475
170 476	**SP**	P	*SR*	HA	50476	56476	79476
170 477	**SP**	P	*SR*	HA	50477	56477	79477
170 478	**SP**	P			50478	56478	79478

Class 170/5. Central Trains 2-car units. DMSL–DMSL.

DMSL(A). Adtranz Derby 1999–2000. –/55 1TD 2W. 45.80 t.
DMSL(B). Adtranz Derby 1999–2000. –/67 1T. 46.80 t.

Advertising Liveries:

170 505 Bullring shopping centre, Birmingham – black and brown with various images.
170 513 Robin Hood Line promotional livery – Lime green, green and red with various images.

170 501	r	**CT**	P	*CT*	TS	50501 79501
170 502	r	**CT**	P	*CT*	TS	50502 79502
170 503	r	**CT**	P	*CT*	TS	50503 79503
170 504	r	**CT**	P	*CT*	TS	50504 79504
170 505	r	**AL**	P	*CT*	TS	50505 79505
170 506	r	**CT**	P	*CT*	TS	50506 79506
170 507	r	**CT**	P	*CT*	TS	50507 79507
170 508	r	**CT**	P	*CT*	TS	50508 79508
170 509	r	**CT**	P	*CT*	TS	50509 79509
170 510	r	**CT**	P	*CT*	TS	50510 79510
170 511	r	**CT**	P	*CT*	TS	50511 79511
170 512	r	**CT**	P	*CT*	TS	50512 79512
170 513	r	**AL**	P	*CT*	TS	50513 79513
170 514	r	**CT**	P	*CT*	TS	50514 79514
170 515	r	**CT**	P	*CT*	TS	50515 79515
170 516	r	**CT**	P	*CT*	TS	50516 79516
170 517	r	**CT**	P	*CT*	TS	50517 79517
170 518	r	**CT**	P	*CT*	TS	50518 79518
170 519	r	**CT**	P	*CT*	TS	50519 79519
170 520	r	**CT**	P	*CT*	TS	50520 79520
170 521	r	**CT**	P	*CT*	TS	50521 79521
170 522	r	**CT**	P	*CT*	TS	50522 79522
170 523	r	**CT**	P	*CT*	TS	50523 79523

Class 170/6. Central Trains 3-car units. DMSL–MS–DMSL.

DMSL(A). Adtranz Derby 2000. –/55 1TD 2W. 45.80 t.
MS. Adtranz Derby 2000. –/74. 43.00 t.
DMSL(B). Adtranz Derby 2000. –/67 1T. 46.80 t.

170 630	r	**CT**	P	*CT*	TS	50630 56630 79630
170 631	r	**CT**	P	*CT*	TS	50631 56631 79631
170 632	r	**CT**	P	*CT*	TS	50632 56632 79632
170 633	r	**CT**	P	*CT*	TS	50633 56633 79633
170 634	r	**CT**	P	*CT*	TS	50634 56634 79634
170 635	r	**CT**	P	*CT*	TS	50635 56635 79635
170 636	r	**CT**	P	*CT*	TS	50636 56636 79636
170 637	r	**CT**	P	*CT*	TS	50637 56637 79637
170 638	r	**CT**	P	*CT*	TS	50638 56638 79638
170 639	r	**CT**	P	*CT*	TS	50639 56639 79639

CLASS 171   TURBOSTAR   BOMBARDIER

DMCL–DMSL or DMCL–MS–MS–DMCL. Southern units. Air conditioned.

Construction: Welded aluminium bodies with bolt-on steel ends.
Engines: One MTU 6R183TD13H of 315 kW (422 h.p.) at 1900 r.p.m.
Transmission: Hydraulic. Voith T211rzze to ZF final drive.
Bogies: One Adtranz P3–23 and one BREL T3–23 per car.
Couplers: Dellner 12.
Seating Layout: 1: 2+1 facing/unidirectional. 2: 2+2 facing/unidirectional.
Dimensions: 23.62 x 2.69 m.
Gangways: Within unit only.   **Wheel Arrangement:** 2-B (– B-2) – B-2.
Doors: Twin-leaf swing plug.   **Maximum Speed:** 100 m.p.h.
Multiple Working: Within class and with EMU Classes 375 and 377 only.

Class 171/7. Southern 2-car units. DMCL–DMSL.

Notes: 171 721–171 726 were built as Class 170s, but renumbered as 171s on fitting with Dellner 12 couplers. 171 727–171 729 are on order.

DMCL. Bombardier Derby 2003–2005. 9/43 1TD 2W.   .   t.
DMSL. Bombardier Derby 2003–2005. –/64 1T.   .   t.

171 721	(170 721)	**SN**	P	*SN*	SU	50721	79721
171 722	(170 722)	**SN**	P	*SN*	SU	50722	79722
171 723	(170 723)	**SN**	P	*SN*	SU	50723	79723
171 724	(170 724)	**SN**	P	*SN*	SU	50724	79724
171 725	(170 725)	**SN**	P	*SN*	SU	50725	79725
171 726	(170 726)	**SN**	P	*SN*	SU	50726	79726
171 727		**SN**	P			50727	79727
171 728		**SN**	P			50728	79728
171 729		**SN**	P			50729	79729

Class 171/8. Southern 4-car units. DMCL(A)–MS–MS–DMCL(B).

DMCL(A). Bombardier Derby 2004. 9/43 1TD 2W.   .   t.
MS. Bombardier Derby 2004. –/74.   .   t.
DMCL(B). Bombardier Derby 2004. 9/50 1T.   .   t.

171 801	**SN**	P	*SN*	SU	50801	54801	56801	79801
171 802	**SN**	P	*SN*	SU	50802	54802	56802	79802
171 803	**SN**	P	*SN*	SU	50803	54803	56803	79803
171 804	**SN**	P	*SN*	SU	50804	54804	56804	79804
171 805	**SN**	P	*SN*	SU	50805	54805	56805	79805
171 806	**SN**	P	*SN*	SU	50806	54806	56806	79806

CLASS 175   CORADIA 1000   ALSTOM

Air Conditioned.

Construction: Steel.
Engines: One Cummins N14 of 335 kW (450 h.p.).
Transmission: Hydraulic. Voith T211rzze to ZF final drive.
Bogies: **Couplers:** Scharfenberg.
Seating Layout: 2+2 facing/unidirectional.
Dimensions: 23.71/23.03 x 2.73 m.
Gangways: Within unit only.   **Wheel Arrangement:** 2-B (– B-2) – B-2.
Doors: Single-leaf swing plug.   **Maximum Speed:** 100 m.p.h.
Multiple Working: Within class and with Class 180.

Note: Although operated by Arriva Trains Wales several Class 175s are hired back to Trans-Pennine Express and First North Western for use on Manchester Airport to Blackpool/Barrow & Millom/Windermere services.

Class 175/0. DMSL–DMSL. 2-car units.

DMSL(A). Alstom Birmingham 1999–2000. –/54 1TD 2W. 51.00 t.
DMSL(B). Alstom Birmingham 1999–2000. –/64 1T. 51.00 t.

175 001	FS	A	AW	CH	50701	79701
175 002	FS	A	AW	CH	50702	79702
175 003	FS	A	AW	CH	50703	79703
175 004	FS	A	AW	CH	50704	79704
175 005	FS	A	AW	CH	50705	79705
175 006	FS	A	AW	CH	50706	79706
175 007	FS	A	AW	CH	50707	79707
175 008	FS	A	AW	CH	50708	79708
175 009	FS	A	AW	CH	50709	79709
175 010	FS	A	AW	CH	50710	79710
175 011	FS	A	AW	CH	50711	79711

Names (carried on one side of each DMSL):

175 004	MENCAP National Colleges Pengwern College
175 006	Brondyffryn Trust
175 008	Valhalla Blackpool Pleasure Beach

Class 175/1. DMSL–MSL–DMSL. 3-car units.

DMSL(A). Alstom Birmingham 1999–2001. –/54 1TD 2W. 51.00 t.
MSL. Alstom Birmingham 1999–2001. –/68 1T. 43 t 68 1T. 47.50 t.
DMSL(B). Alstom Birmingham 1999–2001. –/64 1T. 51.00 t.

175 101	FS	A	AW	CH	50751	56751	79751
175 102	FS	A	AW	CH	50752	56752	79752
175 103	FS	A	AW	CH	50753	56753	79753
175 104	FS	A	AW	CH	50754	56754	79754
175 105	FS	A	AW	CH	50755	56755	79755
175 106	FS	A	AW	CH	50756	56756	79756
175 107	FS	A	AW	CH	50757	56757	79757
175 108	FS	A	AW	CH	50758	56758	79758

175 109	**FS**	A	*AW*	CH	50759	56759	79759
175 110	**FS**	A	*AW*	CH	50760	56760	79760
175 111	**FS**	A	*AW*	CH	50761	56761	79761
175 112	**FS**	A	*AW*	CH	50762	56762	79762
175 113	**FS**	A	*AW*	CH	50763	56763	79763
175 114	**FS**	A	*AW*	CH	50764	56764	79764
175 115	**FS**	A	*AW*	CH	50765	56765	79765
175 116	**FS**	A	*AW*	CH	50766	56766	79766

Names (carried on one side of each DMSL):

175 103	Mum
175 107	CORONATION ST. ROVERS RETURN
175 111	Brief Encounter
175 112	South Lakes Wild Animal Park SUMATRAN TIGER
175 114	Commonwealth Cruiser
175 116	PETER VL JONES Community Rail Officer – Conwy Valley Line

CLASS 180   ADELANTE   ALSTOM

Air Conditioned.

Construction: Steel.
Engines: One Cummins QSK19 of 560 kW (750 h.p.) at 2100 r.p.m.
Transmission: Hydraulic. Voith T312br to Voith final drive.
Bogies: Alstom MB2.
Couplers: Scharfenberg.
Seating Layout: 1: 2+1 facing/unidirectional, 2: 2+2 facing/unidirectional.
Dimensions: 23.71/23.03 x 2.73 m.   **Gangways:** Within unit only.
Wheel Arrangement: 2-B – B-2 – B-2 – B-2.
Doors: Single-leaf swing plug.   **Maximum Speed:** 125 m.p.h.
Multiple Working: Within class and with Class 175.

DMSL(A). Alstom Birmingham 2000–2001. –/46 2W 1TD. 53.00 t.
MFL. Alstom Birmingham 2000–2001. 42/– 1T 1W + catering point. 51.50 t.
MSL. Alstom Birmingham 2000–2001. –/68 1T. 51.50 t.
MSLRB. Alstom Birmingham 2000–2001. –/56 1T. 51.50 t.
DMSL(B). Alstom Birmingham 2000–2001. –/56 1T. 53.00 t.

180 101	**FG**	A	*GW*	OM	50901	54901	55901	56901	59901
180 102	**FG**	A	*GW*	OM	50902	54902	55902	56902	59902
180 103	**FG**	A	*GW*	OM	50903	54903	55903	56903	59903
180 104	**FG**	A	*GW*	OM	50904	54904	55904	56904	59904
180 105	**FG**	A	*GW*	OM	50905	54905	55905	56905	59905
180 106	**FG**	A	*GW*	OM	50906	54906	55906	56906	59906
180 107	**FG**	A	*GW*	OM	50907	54907	55907	56907	59907
180 108	**FG**	A	*GW*	OM	50908	54908	55908	56908	59908
180 109	**FG**	A	*GW*	OM	50909	54909	55909	56909	59909
180 110	**FG**	A	*GW*	OM	50910	54910	55910	56910	59910
180 111	**FG**	A	*GW*	OM	50911	54911	55911	56911	59911
180 112	**FG**	A	*GW*	OM	50912	54912	55912	56912	59912
180 113	**FG**	A	*GW*	OM	50913	54913	55913	56913	59913
180 114	**FG**	A	*GW*	OM	50914	54914	55914	56914	59914

CLASS 185   DESIRO UK   SIEMENS

Air Conditioned.

Construction: Steel.
Engines: One Cummins engine of 560 kW (750 h.p.) at 2100 r.p.m.
Transmission: Voith.
Bogies: Siemens.
Couplers: Dellner 12.
Seating Layout: 1: 2+1 facing/unidirectional, 2: 2+2 facing/unidirectional.
Dimensions:
Gangways: Within unit only.
Wheel Arrangement: 2-B – 2-B – B-2.
Doors: Double-leaf sliding plug.   **Maximum Speed:** 100 m.p.h.
Multiple Working: Within class.

DMCL. Siemens Uerdingen 2004–2006. 15/26 2W 1TD. . t.
MSL. Siemens Uerdingen 2004–2006. –/72 1T. . t.
DMS. Siemens Uerdingen 2004–2006. –/68. . t.

185 101	**FG**	A	51101	53101	54101
185 102	**FG**	A	51102	53102	54102
185 103	**FG**	A	51103	53103	54103
185 104	**FG**	A	51104	53104	54104
185 105	**FG**	A	51105	53105	54105
185 106	**FG**	A	51106	53106	54106
185 107	**FG**	A	51107	53107	54107
185 108	**FG**	A	51108	53108	54108
185 109	**FG**	A	51109	53109	54109
185 110	**FG**	A	51110	53110	54110
185 111	**FG**	A	51111	53111	54111
185 112	**FG**	A	51112	53112	54112
185 113	**FG**	A	51113	53113	54113
185 114	**FG**	A	51114	53114	54114
185 115	**FG**	A	51115	53115	54115
185 116	**FG**	A	51116	53116	54116
185 117	**FG**	A	51117	53117	54117
185 118	**FG**	A	51118	53118	54118
185 119	**FG**	A	51119	53119	54119
185 120	**FG**	A	51120	53120	54120
185 121	**FG**	A	51121	53121	54121
185 122	**FG**	A	51122	53122	54122
185 123	**FG**	A	51123	53123	54123
185 124	**FG**	A	51124	53124	54124
185 125	**FG**	A	51125	53125	54125
185 126	**FG**	A	51126	53126	54126
185 127	**FG**	A	51127	53127	54127
185 128	**FG**	A	51128	53128	54128
185 129	**FG**	A	51129	53129	54129
185 130	**FG**	A	51130	53130	54130
185 131	**FG**	A	51131	53131	54131

185 132	**FG**	A	51132	53132	54132
185 133	**FG**	A	51133	53133	54133
185 134	**FG**	A	51134	53134	54134
185 135	**FG**	A	51135	53135	54135
185 136	**FG**	A	51136	53136	54136
185 137	**FG**	A	51137	53137	54137
185 138	**FG**	A	51138	53138	54138
185 139	**FG**	A	51139	53139	54139
185 140	**FG**	A	51140	53140	54140
185 141	**FG**	A	51141	53141	54141
185 142	**FG**	A	51142	53142	54142
185 143	**FG**	A	51143	53143	54143
185 144	**FG**	A	51144	53144	54144
185 145	**FG**	A	51145	53145	54145
185 146	**FG**	A	51146	53146	54146
185 147	**FG**	A	51147	53147	54147
185 148	**FG**	A	51148	53148	54148
185 149	**FG**	A	51149	53149	54149
185 150	**FG**	A	51150	53150	54150
185 151	**FG**	A	51151	53151	54151

2. DIESEL ELECTRIC UNITS

The following features are standard to ex-BR Southern Region diesel-electric multiple unit power cars (Classes 201–207):

Construction: Steel.
Engine: One English Electric 4SRKT Mk. 2 of 450 kW (600 h.p.) at 850 r.p.m.
Main Generator: English Electric EE824.
Traction Motors: Two English Electric EE507 mounted on the inner bogie.

Bogies: SR Mk. 4. (Former EMU TSL vehicles have Commonwealth bogies).
Couplers: Drophead buckeye.
Doors: Manually operated slam.
Brakes: Electro-pneumatic and automatic air.
Maximum Speed: 75 m.p.h.
Multiple Working: Other ex BR Southern Region DEMU vehicles.

CLASS 201/202 PRESERVED "HASTINGS" UNIT BR

DMBS–2TSL–TSRB–TSL–DMBS.

Preserved unit made up from two Class 201 short-frame cars and three Class 202 long-frame cars. The "Hastings" units were made with narrow body-profiles for use on the section between Tonbridge and Battle which had tunnels of restricted loading gauge. These tunnels were converted to single track operation in the 1980s thus allowing standard loading gauge stock to be used. The set also contains a Class 411 EMU trailer (not Hastings line gauge) and a Class 422 EMU buffet car.

Gangways: Within unit only.
Seating Layout: 2+2 facing.
Dimensions: 18.36 x 2.50 m (60000/60116/60501), 20.34 x 2.50 m. (60118/60529) 20.34 x 2.82 m (69337/70262).

60000. DMBS. Lot No. 30329 Eastleigh 1957. –/22. 54 t.
60116. DMBS (Spare). Lot No. 30395 Eastleigh 1957. –/31. 55 t.
60118. DMBS. Lot No. 30395 Eastleigh 1957. –/30. 55 t.
60501. TSL. Lot No. 30331 Eastleigh 1957. –/52 2T. 29 t.
60529. TSL. Lot No. 30397 Eastleigh 1957. –/60 2T. 30 t.
69337. TSRB (ex Class 422 EMU). Lot No. 30805 York 1970. –/40. 35 t.
70262. TSL (ex Class 411/5 EMU). Lot No. 30455 Eastleigh 1958–1959. –/64 2T. 33.78 t.

201 001	**G**	HD	*HD*	SE	60000	60529	70262	69337	60501
Spare	**G**	HD	*HD*	SE	60116				

Names:

60000 Hastings
60116 Mountfield
60118 Tunbridge Wells

CLASS 205/0 (3H)   BR "HAMPSHIRE"

Southern units due for withdrawal by the end of 2004. DMBS–TSL–DTCsoL or DMBS–DTCsoL.

Gangways: Non-gangwayed.
Seating Layout: 3+2 facing or compartments.
Dimensions: 20.33 x 2.82 m (DMBS), 20.28 x 2.82 m (TS), 20.36 x 2.82 m (DTCsoL).

60108/60154. DMBS. Lot No. 30332 Eastleigh 1957. –/52. 56 t.
60146/60150/60151. DMBS. Lot No. 30671 Eastleigh 1960–1962. –/42. 56 t.
60658. TS. Lot No. 30542 Eastleigh 1958–1959. –/104. 30 t.
60673/60677/60678. TS. Lot No. 30672 Eastleigh 1960–1962. –/104. 30 t.
60800/60808. DTCsoL. Lot No. 30333 Eastleigh 1956–1957. 13/50 2T. 32 t.
60827/60831/60832. DTCsoL. Lot No. 30673 Eastleigh 1960–1962. 13/62 2T. (13/ 60 2T 60827 (DE304), 13/57 2T 60831 (DE305)) 32 t.

205 001	**CX**	P	*SN*	SU	60154		60800
205 009	**CX**	P	*SN*	SU	60108	60658	60808
205 028	**CX**	P	*SN*	SU	60146	60673	60827
205 032	**CX**	P	*SN*	SU	60150	60677	60831
205 033	**CX**	P	*SN*	SU	60151	60678	60832

CLASS 220   VOYAGER   BOMBARDIER

DMS–MSRMB–MS–DMF.

Construction: Steel.
Engine: Cummins of 750 h.p. (560 kW) at 1800 r.p.m.
Transmission: Two Alstom Onix 800 three-phase traction motors of 275 kW.
Braking: Rheostatic and electro-pneumatic.
Bogies: Bombardier B5005.
Couplers: Dellner.
Seating Layout: 1: 2+1 facing/unidirectional, 2: 2+2 mainly unidirectional.
Dimensions: 23.85/22.82 x 2.73 m.
Gangways: Within unit only.
Wheel Arrangement: 1A-A1 – 1A-A1 – 1A-A1 – 1A-A1.
Doors: Single-leaf swing plug.
Maximum Speed: 125 m.p.h.
Multiple Working: Within class and with Classes 221 and 222. Also with Dellner coupler-fitted Class 57 locomotives.

DMS. Bombardier Brugge/Wakefield 2000–2001. –/42 1TD 1W. 48.10 t.
MSRMB. Bombardier Brugge/Wakefield 2000–2001. –/58. 48.00 t.
MS. Bombardier Brugge/Wakefield 2000–2001. –/60 1TD 1W. 45.00 t.
DMF. Bombardier Brugge/Wakefield 2000–2001. 26/– 1TD 1W. 44.50 t.

220 001	**VT**	HX	*VX*	CZ	60301	60701	60201	60401
220 002	**VT**	HX	*VX*	CZ	60302	60702	60202	60402
220 003	**VT**	HX	*VX*	CZ	60303	60703	60203	60403
220 004	**VT**	HX	*VX*	CZ	60304	60704	60204	60404

220 005	**VT**	HX	_VX_	CZ	60305	60705	60205	60405
220 006	**VT**	HX	_VX_	CZ	60306	60706	60206	60406
220 007	**VT**	HX	_VX_	CZ	60307	60707	60207	60407
220 008	**VT**	HX	_VX_	CZ	60308	60708	60208	60408
220 009	**VT**	HX	_VX_	CZ	60309	60709	60209	60409
220 010	**VT**	HX	_VX_	CZ	60310	60710	60210	60410
220 011	**VT**	HX	_VX_	CZ	60311	60711	60211	60411
220 012	**VT**	HX	_VX_	CZ	60312	60712	60212	60412
220 013	**VT**	HX	_VX_	CZ	60313	60713	60213	60413
220 014	**VT**	HX	_VX_	CZ	60314	60714	60214	60414
220 015	**VT**	HX	_VX_	CZ	60315	60715	60215	60415
220 016	**VT**	HX	_VX_	CZ	60316	60716	60216	60416
220 017	**VT**	HX	_VX_	CZ	60317	60717	60217	60417
220 018	**VT**	HX	_VX_	CZ	60318	60718	60218	60418
220 019	**VT**	HX	_VX_	CZ	60319	60719	60219	60419
220 020	**VT**	HX	_VX_	CZ	60320	60720	60220	60420
220 021	**VT**	HX	_VX_	CZ	60321	60721	60221	60421
220 022	**VT**	HX	_VX_	CZ	60322	60722	60222	60422
220 023	**VT**	HX	_VX_	CZ	60323	60723	60223	60423
220 024	**VT**	HX	_VX_	CZ	60324	60724	60224	60424
220 025	**VT**	HX	_VX_	CZ	60325	60725	60225	60425
220 026	**VT**	HX	_VX_	CZ	60326	60726	60226	60426
220 027	**VT**	HX	_VX_	CZ	60327	60727	60227	60427
220 028	**VT**	HX	_VX_	CZ	60328	60728	60228	60428
220 029	**VT**	HX	_VX_	CZ	60329	60729	60229	60429
220 030	**VT**	HX	_VX_	CZ	60330	60730	60230	60430
220 031	**VT**	HX	_VX_	CZ	60331	60731	60231	60431
220 032	**VT**	HX	_VX_	CZ	60332	60732	60232	60432
220 033	**VT**	HX	_VX_	CZ	60333	60733	60233	60433
220 034	**VT**	HX	_VX_	CZ	60334	60734	60234	60434

Names (carried on MS):

220 001	Somerset Voyager	220 019	Mersey Voyager
220 002	Forth Voyager	220 020	Wessex Voyager
220 003	Solent Voyager	220 021	Staffordshire Voyager
220 004	Cumbrian Voyager	220 022	Brighton Voyager
220 005	Guildford Voyager	220 023	Mancunian Voyager
220 006	Clyde Voyager	220 024	Sheffield Voyager
220 007	Thames Voyager	220 025	Severn Voyager
220 008	Draig Gymreig/Welsh Dragon	220 026	Stagecoach Voyager
220 009	Gatwick Voyager	220 027	Avon Voyager
220 010	Ribble Voyager	220 028	Black Country Voyager
220 011	Tyne Voyager	220 029	Vyajer Kernewek/
220 012	Lanarkshire Voyager		Cornish Voyager
220 013	Gwibiwr De Cymru/South	220 030	Devon Voyager
	Wales Voyager	220 031	Tay Voyager
220 014	South Yorkshire Voyager	220 032	Grampian Voyager
220 015	Solway Voyager	220 033	Fife Voyager
220 016	Midland Voyager	220 034	Yorkshire Voyager
220 017	BOMBARDIER Voyager		
220 018	Dorset Voyager		

▲ Thames Trains-liveried 166 219 (now with First Group brandings as TT are now known as First Great Western Link) arrives at Guildford on 04/09/04 with the 10.34 Reading–Gatwick Airport. **Robert Pritchard**

▼ 168 005 pauses at Banbury on 21/08/04 with the 08.40 Marylebone–Birmingham Snow Hill. **Mark Beal**

▲ 170 202, in the slightly revised "One" livery (the grey is lighter and has a blue tinge) leaves Stowmarket on 28/07/04 with the 15.13 Cambridge–Ipswich.
Gavin Morrison

▼ 170 431 is seen at Inverkeithing on 06/07/04 with the 14.08 Dyce–Edinburgh Waverley.
Steve Taylor

Hull Trains 170 393 is seen at Marholm, north of Peterborough, with a King's Cross–Hull service on 30/07/04. These units are due to transfer to First ScotRail in Spring 2005.

John Rudd

▲ Southern-liveried 171 802 is seen at Derby on 14/06/04, prior to delivery to Selhurst for Southern use. **Gavin Morrison**

▼ Although still all in First Group livery, most 175s are now operated by Arriva Trains Wales, with some also used by Trans-Pennine Express. Here 175 108 passes Rhyl Marine Lake with the 09.50 Holyhead–Crewe on 29/07/04. **Robert Pritchard**

▲ 180 106 is seen at Goring with the 09.55 Cardiff–Paddington First Great Western service of 25/10/03.　　　　**Rodney Lissenden**

▼ "Hastings" DEMU 1001 was frequently used as cover for Class 205/207 "Thumpers" and new Southern Class 170s on the Ashford–Hastings "Marshlink" line in 2004. On 17/06/04 it leaves Rye with the 11.24 from Ashford.　　**Ian Feather**

▲ Virgin Trains-liveried 220 022 "Brighton Voyager" is seen at Beckfoot with the 07.20 Aberdeen–Bournemouth on 18/03/03. **Chris Booth**

▼ 221 103 "Christopher Columbus" passes The Chevin, Derbyshire with the 06.35 Edinburgh–Bristol on 23/10/03. **Paul Robertson**

New Midland Mainline 4-car "Meridian" 222 009 passes Breaston 02/09/04 with a Derby–St. Pancras stopping service.
Jon Barlow

▲ Maroon-liveried Sandite unit 960 010 (977858/55024) is seen at Aylesbury station on 19/08/04. **Paul Shannon**

▼ Test Unit "Iris 2" 901 002 in Network Rail yellow livery is seen at Milton Keynes Central on 08/04/04. **Mark Beal**

CLASS 221   SUPER VOYAGER   BOMBARDIER

DMS–MSRMB–MS(–MS)–DMF. Tilting units.

Construction: Steel.
Engine: Cummins of 750 h.p. (560 kW) at 1800 r.p.m.
Transmission: Two Alstom Onix 800 three-phase traction motors of 275 kW.
Braking: Rheostatic and electro-pneumatic.
Bogies: Bombardier HVP.
Couplers: Dellner.
Seating Layout: 1: 2+1 facing/unidirectional, 2: 2+2 mainly unidirectional.
Dimensions: 23.85/22.82 x 2.73 m.
Gangways: Within unit only.
Wheel Arrangement: 1A-A1 – 1A-A1 – 1A-A1 (– 1A-A1) – 1A-A1.
Doors: Single-leaf swing plug.
Maximum Speed: 125 m.p.h.
Multiple Working: Within class and with Classes 220 and 222. Also with Dellner coupler-fitted Class 57 locomotives.

DMS. Bombardier Brugge/Wakefield 2001–2002. –/42 1TD 1W. 58.30 t.
MSRMB. Bombardier Brugge/Wakefield 2001–2002. –/58. 58.00 t.
MS. Bombardier Brugge/Wakefield 2001–2002. –/60 1TD 1W. 55.80 t.
DMF. Bombardier Brugge/Wakefield 2001–2002. 26/– 1TD 1W. 54.90 t.

221 101	**VT**	HX	*VX*	CZ	60351	60751	60951	60851	60451
221 102	**VT**	HX	*VX*	CZ	60352	60752	60952	60852	60452
221 103	**VT**	HX	*VX*	CZ	60353	60753	60953	60853	60453
221 104	**VT**	HX	*VX*	CZ	60354	60754	60954	60854	60454
221 105	**VT**	HX	*VX*	CZ	60355	60755	60955	60855	60455
221 106	**VT**	HX	*VX*	CZ	60356	60756	60956	60856	60456
221 107	**VT**	HX	*VX*	CZ	60357	60757	60957	60857	60457
221 108	**VT**	HX	*VX*	CZ	60358	60758	60958	60858	60458
221 109	**VT**	HX	*VX*	CZ	60359	60759	60959	60859	60459
221 110	**VT**	HX	*VX*	CZ	60360	60760	60960	60860	60460
221 111	**VT**	HX	*VX*	CZ	60361	60761	60961	60861	60461
221 112	**VT**	HX	*VX*	CZ	60362	60762	60962	60862	60462
221 113	**VT**	HX	*VX*	CZ	60363	60763	60963	60863	60463
221 114	**VT**	HX	*VX*	CZ	60364	60764	60964	60864	60464
221 115	**VT**	HX	*VX*	CZ	60365	60765	60965	60865	60465
221 116	**VT**	HX	*VX*	CZ	60366	60766	60966	60866	60466
221 117	**VT**	HX	*VX*	CZ	60367	60767	60967	60867	60467
221 118	**VT**	HX	*VX*	CZ	60368	60768	60968	60868	60468
221 119	**VT**	HX	*VX*	CZ	60369	60769	60969	60869	60469
221 120	**VT**	HX	*VX*	CZ	60370	60770	60970	60870	60470
221 121	**VT**	HX	*VX*	CZ	60371	60771	60971	60871	60471
221 122	**VT**	HX	*VX*	CZ	60372	60772	60972	60872	60472
221 123	**VT**	HX	*VX*	CZ	60373	60773	60973	60873	60473
221 124	**VT**	HX	*VX*	CZ	60374	60774	60974	60874	60474
221 125	**VT**	HX	*VX*	CZ	60375	60775	60975	60875	60475
221 126	**VT**	HX	*VX*	CZ	60376	60776	60976	60876	60476
221 127	**VT**	HX	*VX*	CZ	60377	60777	60977	60877	60477

221 128	**VT**	HX	*VX*	CZ	60378	60778	60978	60878	60478
221 129	**VT**	HX	*VX*	CZ	60379	60779	60979	60879	60479
221 130	**VT**	HX	*VX*	CZ	60380	60780	60980	60880	60480
221 131	**VT**	HX	*VX*	CZ	60381	60781	60981	60881	60481
221 132	**VT**	HX	*VX*	CZ	60382	60782	60982	60882	60482
221 133	**VT**	HX	*VX*	CZ	60383	60783	60983	60883	60483
221 134	**VT**	HX	*VX*	CZ	60384	60784	60984	60884	60484
221 135	**VT**	HX	*VX*	CZ	60385	60785	60985	60885	60485
221 136	**VT**	HX	*VX*	CZ	60386	60786	60986	60886	60486
221 137	**VT**	HX	*VX*	CZ	60387	60787	60987	60887	60487
221 138	**VT**	HX	*VX*	CZ	60388	60788	60988	60888	60488
221 139	**VT**	HX	*VX*	CZ	60389	60789	60989	60889	60489
221 140	**VT**	HX	*VX*	CZ	60390	60790	60990	60890	60490
221 141	**VT**	HX	*VX*	CZ	60391	60791	60991		60491
221 142	**VT**	HX	*VX*	CZ	60392	60792	60992		60492
221 143	**VT**	HX	*VX*	CZ	60393	60793	60993		60493
221 144	**VT**	HX	*VX*	CZ	60394	60794	60994		60494

Names (carried on MS No. 609xx):

221 101	Louis Bleriot	221 123	Henry Hudson
221 102	John Cabot	221 124	Charles Lindbergh
221 103	Christopher Columbus	221 125	Henry the Navigator
221 104	Sir John Franklin	221 126	Captain Robert Scott
221 105	William Baffin	221 127	Wright Brothers
221 106	Willem Barents	221 128	Captain John Smith
221 107	Sir Martin Frobisher	221 129	George Vancouver
221 108	Sir Ernest Shackleton	221 130	Michael Palin
221 109	Marco Polo	221 131	Edgar Evans
221 110	James Cook	221 132	William Speirs Bruce
221 111	Roald Amundsen	221 133	Alexander Selkirk
221 112	Ferdinand Magellan	221 134	Mary Kingsley
221 113	Sir Walter Raleigh	221 135	Donald Campbell
221 114	Sir Francis Drake	221 136	Yuri Gagarin
221 115	Sir Francis Chichester	221 137	Mayflower Pilgrims
221 116	David Livingstone	221 138	Thor Heyerdahl
221 117	Sir Henry Morton Stanley	221 139	Leif Erikson
221 118	Mungo Park	221 140	Vasco da Gama
221 119	Amelia Earhart	221 141	Amerigo Vespucci
221 120	Amy Johnson	221 142	Matthew Flinders
221 121	Charles Darwin	221 143	Auguste Picard
221 122	Doctor Who	221 144	Prince Madoc

CLASS 222   MERIDIAN   BOMBARDIER

Construction: Steel.
Engine: Cummins of 750 h.p. (560 kW) at 1800 r.p.m.
Transmission: Two Alstom Onix 800 three-phase traction motors of 275 kW.
Braking: Rheostatic and electro-pneumatic.
Bogies: Bombardier B5005.
Couplers: Dellner.
Seating Layout: 1: 2+1, 2: 2+2 facing/unidirectional.
Dimensions: 23.85/22.82 x 2.73 m.
Gangways: Within unit only.
Wheel Arrangement: All cars 1A-A1.
Doors: Single-leaf swing plug.
Maximum Speed: 125 m.p.h.
Multiple Working: Within class and with Classes 220 and 221.

222 001–222 007. DMRFO–MFO–MFO–MSO–MSO–MSORMB–MSO–MSO–
DMSO. 9-car units. Ordered for Midland Mainline but now not required. Ultimate
operator at present unknown!

DMRFO. Bombardier Brugge 2004–2005. 22/– 1TD 1W. 49.99 t.
MFO. Bombardier Brugge 2004–2005. 42/– 1T. 48.2 t.
MSO. Bombardier Brugge 2004–2005. –/70 1T. 48.6 t.
MSORMB. Bombardier Brugge 2004–2005. –/62. 47.93 t.
DMSO. Bombardier Brugge 2004–2005. –/40 1TD 1W. 51.0 t.

222 001	**MN**	H	60241	60341	60441	60621	60561
			60551	60541	60531	60161	
222 002	**MN**	H	60242	60342	60442	60622	60562
			60552	60542	60532	60162	
222 003	**MN**	H	60243	60343	60443	60623	60563
			60553	60543	60533	60163	
222 004		H	60244	60344	60444	60624	60564
			60554	60544	60534	60164	
222 005		H	60245	60345	60445	60625	60565
			60555	60545	60535	60165	
222 006		H	60246	60346	60446	60626	60566
			60556	60546	60536	60166	
222 007		H	60247	60347	60447	60627	60567
			60557	60547	60537	60167	

222 008–222 023. DMRFO–MCO–MSORMB–DMSO. Midland Mainline 4-car units.

DMRFO. Bombardier Brugge 2003–2004. 22/– 1TD 1W. 49.99 t.
MCO. Bombardier Brugge 2003–2004. 28/22 1T. 47.04 t.
MSORMB. Bombardier Brugge 2003–2004. –/62. 47.93 t.
DMSO. Bombardier Brugge 2003–2004. –/40 1TD 1W. 51.0 t.

222 008	**MN**	H	*MM*	CZ	60248	60918	60628	60168
222 009	**MN**	H	*MM*	CZ	60249	60919	60629	60169
222 010	**MN**	H	*MM*	CZ	60250	60920	60630	60170
222 011	**MN**	H	*MM*	CZ	60251	60921	60631	60171
222 012	**MN**	H	*MM*	CZ	60252	60922	60632	60172

222 013	MN	H	MM	CZ	60253	60923	60633	60173
222 014	MN	H	MM	CZ	60254	60924	60634	60174
222 015	MN	H	MM	CZ	60255	60925	60635	60175
222 016	MN	H	MM	CZ	60256	60926	60636	60176
222 017	MN	H	MM	CZ	60257	60927	60637	60177
222 018	MN	H	MM	CZ	60258	60928	60638	60178
222 019	MN	H	MM	CZ	60259	60929	60639	60179
222 020	MN	H	MM	CZ	60260	60930	60640	60180
222 021	MN	H	MM	CZ	60261	60931	60641	60181
222 022	MN	H	MM	CZ	60262	60932	60642	60182
222 023	MN	H	MM	CZ	60263	60933	60643	60183

222 101–222 104. DMRFO–MSORMB–MSO–DMSO. 4-car units under construction for Hull Trains.

DMRFO. Bombardier Brugge 2005. 22/– 1TD 1W.   . t.
MSO. Bombardier Brugge 2005. –/70 1T.   . t.
MSORMB. Bombardier Brugge 2005. –/62.   . t.
DMSO. Bombardier Brugge 2005. –/40 1TD 1W.   . t.

222 101	H	60271	60571	60681	60191
222 102	H	60272	60572	60682	60192
222 103	H	60273	60573	60683	60193
222 104	H	60274	60574	60684	60194

3. SERVICE DMUS

This section lists vehicles not used for passenger-carrying purposes. Some vehicles are numbered in the special service stock number series.

CLASS 901   ULTRASONIC TEST UNIT

DM–DM. Converted 1986 from Class 101. Gangwayed within unit. Often operates with either Overhead Line Equipment Test Coach 975091 (see Coaching Stock Pocket Book) or 999602 (see below) as a centre car.

Construction: Aluminium alloy body on steel underframe.
Engines: Two Leyland 680/1 of 112 kW (150 h.p.) at 1800 r.p.m. per power car.
Transmission: Mechanical. Cardan shaft and freewheel to a four-speed epicyclic gearbox with a further cardan shaft to the final drive, each engine driving the inner axle of one bogie.
Brakes: Air.
Couplers: Screw couplings.
Brakes: Air.
Doors: Manually-operated slam.

Bogies: DD15 (motor) and DT11 (trailer).
Maximum Speed: 70 m.p.h.
Dimensions: 18.49 x 2.82 m.

Multiple Working: 'Blue Square' coupling code. First generation vehicles may be coupled together to work in multiple up to a maximum of 6 motor cars or 12 cars in total in a formation. First generation vehicles may not be coupled in multiple with second generation vehicles.

977391. DM. Lot No. 30500 Metro-Cammell. 1959. 32.5 t.
977392. DM. Lot No. 30254 Metro-Cammell. 1956. 32.5 t.

901 001   **Y**   NR *SO*   ZA   977391   (51433)   977392   (53167)

CLASS 901 ULTRASONIC TEST UNIT (ADDITIONAL VEHICLE)

T. Converted 1986 from Class 432 EMU. Gangwayed. Operates with 977391/ 977392 (see above).

Construction: Steel.
Bogies: SR Mk. 6.
Brakes: Twin pipe vacuum.
Doors: Manually operated slam.

Maximum Speed: 70 m.p.h.
Couplings: Screw.
Multiple Working: Blue Square.
Dimensions: 19.66 x 2.82 m.

999602. T. Lot No. 30862 York 1974. 55.5 t.

-      **Y**   NR *SO*   ZA   999602   (62483)

CLASS 901   TEST UNIT (Iris 2)

DM–DM. Converted 1991 from Class 101. Gangwayed within unit.

For details see above.

977693. DM. Lot No. 30261 Metro-Cammell. 1957. 32.5 t.
977694. DM. Lot No. 30276 Metro-Cammell. 1958. 32.5 t.

901 002   **Y**   NR *SO*   DF   977693   (53222)   977694   (53338)

CLASS 930   SANDITE/DE-ICING UNIT

DMB–T–DMB. Converted 1993 from Class 205. Gangwayed within unit. Sandite Trailer 977870 is replaced by De-icing trailer 977364 (see below) as required.

Construction: Steel.
Engine: One English Electric 4SRKT Mk. 2 of 450 kW (600 h.p.) at 850 r.p.m.
Transmission: Electric. Two English Electric EE507 traction motors mounted on the bogie at the non-driving end of each power car.
Maximum Speed: 75 m.p.h.   **Bogies:** SR Mk. 4.
Brakes: Electro-pneumatic and automatic air.
Doors: Manually operated slam.   **Couplings:** Drophead buckeye.
Multiple Working: Classes 201–207.
Dimensions: 20.33 x 2.82 x 3.87 m. (DMB); 20.28 x 2.82 m.

977939–977940. DMB. Lot No. 30671 Eastleigh 1962. 56.0 t.
977870. T. Lot No. 30542 Eastleigh 1960. 30.5 t.

930 301	RO	NR	SN	SU	977939	(60145)	977870	(60660)
					977940	(60149)		

UNCLASSIFIED   DE-ICING UNIT

T. Converted 1960 from 4-Sub EMU vehicle. Non gangwayed. Operates with 977939/977940 (see above) in place of Sandite Trailer 977870.

Construction: Steel.
Maximum Speed: 70 m.p.h.   **Couplings:** Drophead buckeye.
Bogies: Central 43 inch.   **Multiple Working:** SR system.
Brakes: Electro-pneumatic and automatic air.
Doors: Manually operated slam.   **Dimensions:** 19.99 x 2.74 m.

977364. T. Southern Railway Eastleigh 1946. 29.0 t.

-	RO	NR	SN	SU	977364	(10400)

CLASS 950   TRACK ASSESSMENT UNIT

DM–DM. Purpose built service unit. Gangwayed within unit.

Construction: Steel.
Engine: One Cummins NT-855-RT5 of 213 kW (285 h.p.) at 2100 r.p.m. per power car.
Transmission: Hydraulic. Voith T211r with cardan shafts to Gmeinder GM190 final drive.
Maximum Speed: 75 m.p.h.   **Couplers:** BSI automatic.
Bogies: BP38 (powered), BT38 (non-powered).
Brakes: Electro-pneumatic.   **Dimensions:** 20.06 x 2.82 m.
Doors: Manually operated slam & power operated sliding.
Multiple Working: Classes 142, 143, 144, 150, 153, 155, 156, 158, 159, 170.

999600. DM. Lot No. 4060 BREL York 1987. 36.5 t.
999601. DM. Lot No. 4061 BREL York 1987. 36.5 t.

950 001	RK	NR	SO	ZA	999600	999601

CLASS 960   SANDITE & SERVICE UNITS

DMB. Converted 1991/1993 from Class 121. Non gangwayed.

For details see Page 10.

960 011 is a Video Survey Units.
960 012 is to undergo conversion for South West Trains, for use as a Route Learning Unit.
960 014 is now a Route Learning Unit.

977723. DMB. Lot No. 30518 Pressed Steel 1960. 38.0 t.
977858–60/66/73. DMB. Lot No. 30518 Pressed Steel 1960. 38.0 t.

960 010	**M**	NR	*CR*	AL	977858	(55024)
960 011	**RK**	NR	*BB*	AP	977859	(55025)
960 012	**RK**	SW		CP	977860	(55028)
960 013	**N**	NR		AL	977866	(55030)
960 014	**BG**	NR	*CR*	AL	977873	(55022)
960 021	**RO**	NR	*CR*	AL	977723	(55021)

CLASS 960   SANDITE UNIT

DMB. Converted 1991 from Class 122. Non gangwayed.

Construction: Steel.
Engines: Two Leyland 1595 of 112 kW (150 h.p.) at 1800 r.p.m.
Transmission: Mechanical. Cardan shaft and freewheel to a four-speed epicyclic gearbox with a further cardan shaft to the final drive, each engine driving the inner axle of one bogie.
Maximum Speed: 70 m.p.h.
Bogies: DD10.   **Couplings:** Screw.
Brakes: Twin pipe vacuum.   **Multiple Working:** Blue Square.
Doors: Manually operated slam.   **Dimensions:** 20.45 x 2.82 m.

975042. DMB. Lot No. 30419 Gloucester 1958. 36.5 t.

960 015	**Y**	NR	*CR*	AL	975042	(55019)

CLASS 960   3-CAR WATER-JETTING UNIT

DMB–IMV–DMB. Converted 2003/04 from Class 117. Non gangwayed.

Construction: Steel.
Engines: Two Leyland 1595 of 112 kW (150 h.p.) at 1800 r.p.m.
Transmission: Mechanical. Cardan shaft and freewheel to a four-speed epicyclic gearbox with a further cardan shaft to the final drive, each engine driving the inner axle of one bogie.
Maximum Speed: 70 m.p.h.
Bogies: DD10.   **Couplings:** Screw.
Brakes: Twin pipe vacuum.   **Multiple Working:** Blue Square.
Doors: Manually operated slam.   **Dimensions:** 20.45 x 2.82 m.

977987/977988. DMB. Lot No. 30419 Gloucester 1958. 36.5 t.
977992. IMV (Intermedite Motor Vehicle). Lot No. 30419 Gloucester 1958. 36.5 t.

960 301	**G**	CR	*CR*	AL	977987	(51371)	977992 (51375)
					977988	(51413)	

CLASS 960   EMERGENCY TRAIN UNITS

Converted from Class 121. Severn Tunnel Emergency Train units.

For details see Page 10.

DMB. Lot No. 30518 Pressed Steel 1960. 38.5 t.

960 302	**Y**	NR	*E*	Sudbrook	977975	(55027)
960 303	**Y**	NR	*E*	Sudbrook	977976	(55031)

CLASS 960   DRIVER TRAINING UNIT

Converted from Class 121.

For details see Page 10.

977968. DMB.

-		**ES**	CA	*CA*	RU	977968 (55029)

CLASS 960   TRACK ASSESSMENT/RECORDING UNIT

DM–DM. Universal track recording unit for video inspections, for measuring rail profiles etc. Plasser type UFM 160-1. Full details awaited.

Construction:	**Engine:**
Transmission:	
Maximum Speed: 100 m.p.h.	**Weight:** 70 t.
Brakes:	**Dimensions:** 20.06 x 2.82 m.

999700. DM. Austria 2000.
999701. DM. Austria 2000.

-	**ES**	ES	*CA*	RU	999700 999701

CLASS 960   TRACK ASSESSMENT/RECORDING UNIT

DM. Full details awaited. Plasser & Theurer EM-SA+ RT100 Survey Cars. Not yet registered for Network Rail use.

Construction:	**Engine:**
Transmission:	
Maximum Speed: 55 m.p.h.	**Weight:** 57 t.
Brakes:	**Dimensions:** 17.70 x 2.75 m.

999800/1. DM. Austria 2000.

	ES	NR	RU	999800
	ES	NR	RU	999801

4. DMUS AWAITING DISPOSAL

The list below comprises vehicles awaiting disposal which are stored on the Network Rail network, together with vehicles stored at other locations which, although awaiting disposal, remain Network Rail registered.
IMPORTANT NOTE: DMUs already at scrapyards are not included in this list.

Class 101

101 676	**RR**	A	PY	51205	51803			
101 678	**RR**	A	PY	51210	53746			
101 680	**RR**	A	PY	53204	51511			
101 685	**G**	A	PY	53164	53160			
101 693	**S**	A	PY	51192	53266			

Note: All vehicles below are classed as "spare" because all sets have in practise been split at their respective storage locations.

Spare	**RR**	A	PY	51189	51432	51496	51498	51506	54055
				54061	54347	54365	54393		
Spare	**S**	A	PY	51188	51231	51247	51435	51500	53268
Spare	**RR**	X	LG	54056					
Spare	**BG**	X	NL	54342					

Class 114

Non-Standard Livery: Grey, red & yellow.

-	**0**	X	TE	977775 (55928)	977776 (54904)

Class 117

Note: All vehicles below are classed as "spare" because all sets have in practise been split at their respective storage locations.

Spare	**RR**	A	PY	59500	59509		
Spare	**N**	A	PY	51350	51366	51383	51408
Spare	**RR**	CR	AL	51411			

Class 122

-	**LH**	E	TE	977941 (55012)

Class 165

Spare	**NT**	A	ZC	58930

Class 205

205 012	**CX**	P	SU	60111		60811
205 018	**CX**	P	SU	60117	60674	60828
205 205	**CX**	P	SU	60110		60810
Spare	**N**	AM	ZG	60650		

Class 951

Spare	**N**	AM	ZG	977696 (60522)

5. CODES

5.1. LIVERY CODES

Code	Description
1	"One" (metallic grey with a broad black bodyside stripe. Pink, yellow, grey, pale green and light blue stripes at the unit/vehicle ends)
AL	Advertising livery (see class heading for details).
AN	Anglia Railways Class 170s (white & turquoise with blue vignette).
AR	Anglia Railways (turquoise blue with a white stripe).
AV	Arriva Trains (turquoise blue with white doors with a cream "swish")
BG	BR blue & grey lined out in white.
BI	"Visit Bristol" promotional livery (deep blue with various images).
CO	Centro (grey/green with light blue, white & yellow stripes).
CR	Chiltern Railways (blue & white with a thin red stripe).
CT	Central Trains (two-tone green with yellow doors. Blue flash and red strpe at vehicle ends).
CX	Connex (white with yellow lower body & blue solebar).
DC	Scenic lines of Devon & Cornwall promotional livery (black with gold cantrail stripe).
ES	Eurailscout GB (Light orange with a blue and purple logo).
FG	First Group corporate Inter-City livery (indigo blue with a white roof & gold, pink & white stripes).
FS	First Group corporate regional/suburban livery (indigo blue with pink & white stripes).
G	BR Southern Region/SR or BR DMU green.
GP	Ginsters Cornish Pasties promotional livery (Black & red with various images and cartoons etc.)
HW	Heart of Wales Line promotional livery (orange with yellow doors).
HT	Hull Trains (white with a broad green band on the lower bodyside).
LH	BR Loadhaul (black with orange cabsides).
M	BR maroon (Maroon lined out in straw & black).
MM	Old Midland Mainline (Teal green with cream lower body sides & three orange stripes).
MN	New Midland Mainline (Thin tangerine stripe on the lower bodyside, ocean blue, grey & white).
MY	Revised Merseytravel (yellow/white with grey stripe).
N	BR Network SouthEast (white & blue with red lower bodyside stripe, grey solebar & cab ends).
NS	Northern Spirit (turquoise blue with lime green "N").
NT	BR Network SouthEast (white & blue with red lower bodyside & cantrail stripes).
NW	North West Trains (blue with gold cantrail stripe & star).
O	Non standard livery (see class heading for details).
P	Porterbrook Leasing Company (purple & grey or white).
PS	Provincial Services (dark blue/grey with light blue & white stripes).
RE	Provincial Services/Regional Railways Express (light grey/buff/dark grey with white, dark blue & light blue stripes).

RK	New Railtrack (green & blue).
RN	North West Regional Railways (dark blue/grey with green & white stripes).
RO	Old Railtrack (orange with white & grey stripes).
RR	Regional Railways (dark blue/grey with light blue & white stripes, three narrow dark blue stripes at vehicle ends).
S	Old Strathclyde PTE (orange & black lined out in white).
SC	New Strathclyde PTE (carmine & cream lined out in black & gold).
SL	Silverlink (indigo blue with white stripe, green lower body & yellow doors).
SN	Southern (white & dark green with light green semi-circles at one end of each vehicle. Light grey band at solebar level.)
SP	New Strathclyde PTE {Class 334 style} (carmine & cream, with a turquoise stripe).
SR	ScotRail (white, terracotta, purple & aquamarine).
SW	South West Trains {long-distance stock} (white & dark blue with black window surrounds, red doors & red panel with orange stripe at unit ends).
TP	First/Keolis Trans-Pennine Express (Plum with a yellow "N" and First Group indigo blue lower bodyside band).
TT	Thames Trains (blue with lime green doors).
VL	Valley Lines (dark green & red with white & light green stripes. Light green doors).
VT	New Virgin Trains (silver, with black window surrounds, white cantrail stripe & red roof. Red swept down at unit ends. Black and white striped doors).
VW	Visit Wales promotional livery (green & red with various images).
WB	Wales & Borders Alphaline (metallic silver with blue doors).
WE	Wessex Trains Alphaline promotional livery (metallic silver with various images, pink doors).
WT	Wessex Trains Alphaline (metallic silver with maroon or pink doors).
WX	Heart of Wessex Line promotional livery (cerise pink).
WY	Old West Yorkshire PTE (red/cream with thin yellow stripe).
WZ	Wessex Trains claret promotional livery with various images. Plain yellow.
YP	New West Yorkshire PTE (red with grey semi-circles).

5.2. OWNER CODES

A	Angel Train Contracts
AM	Alstom
BC	Bridgend County Borough Council
CA	Carillion Rail
CR	Chiltern Railways
E	English Welsh & Scottish Railway
ES	Eurailscout GB
H	HSBC Rail (UK) Ltd.
HD	Hastings Diesels Ltd.
HX	Halifax Asset Finance Ltd.
NR	Network Rail
P	Porterbrook Leasing Company
RD	Rhondda Cynon Taff District Council
RI	Rail Assets Investments Ltd.
SW	South West Trains
X	Sold for scrap/further use and awaiting collection or owner unknown

5.3. OPERATOR CODES

1A	One Anglia
AN	Arriva Trains Northern
AW	Arriva Trains Wales
BB	Balfour Beatty Rail
CA	Carillion Rail
CR	Chiltern Railways
CT	Central Trains
E	English Welsh & Scottish Railway
FK	First Great Western Link
GW	First Great Western
HD	Hastings Diesels
HT	Hull Trains
MM	Midland Mainline
NW	First North Western
SL	Silverlink
SN	Southern
SO	Serco Railtest
SR	First ScotRail
SW	South West Trains
TP	First/Keolis Trans-Pennine Express
VX	Virgin Cross-Country
WX	Wessex Trains

5.4. ALLOCATION & LOCATION CODES

Code	Location	Operator
AL	Aylesbury	Chiltern Railways
AP*	Ashford Rail Plant	Balfour Beatty Rail Plant
BY	Bletchley	Silverlink
CF	Cardiff Canton	Arriva Trains Wales/EWS
CH	Chester	Arriva Trains Wales
CK	Corkerhill (Glasgow)	First ScotRail
CP	Crewe Carriage	London & North Western Railway
CZ	Central Rivers (Burton)	Bombardier Transportation
DF	Derby RTC	Fragonset Railways
DY	Derby Etches Park	Maintrain
EX	Exeter	Wessex Trains
HA	Haymarket (Edinburgh)	First ScotRail
HT	Heaton (Newcastle)	Arriva Trains Northern
IL	Ilford (London)	One Great Eastern
IS	Inverness	First ScotRail
LG	Longsight (Manchester)	First North Western
NC	Norwich Crown Point	One Anglia
NH	Newton Heath (Manchester)	First North Western
NL	Neville Hill (Leeds)	Arriva Trains Northern/Maintrain
OM	Old Oak Common carriage(London)	First Great Western/Riviera Trains
PY	MoD DERA Pig's Bay (Shoeburyness)	Ministry of Defence
RG	Reading	First Great Western Link
RU*	Rugby Rail Plant	Carillion Rail Plant
SA	Salisbury	South West Trains
SE	St. Leonards (Hastings)	St. Leonards Railway Engineering
SU	Selhurst (Croydon)	Southern
TE	Thornaby (Middlesbrough)	EWS
TS	Tyseley (Birmingham)	Maintrain
ZA	RTC Business Park (Derby)	Serco/AEA Technology
ZB	Doncaster Works	Wabtec
ZC	Crewe Works	Bombardier Transportation
ZD	Derby Litchurch Lane Works	Bombardier Transportation
ZF	Doncaster Works (closed)	Bombardier Transportation
ZG	Eastleigh Works	Alstom
ZH	Springburn Works Glasgow	Alstom
ZI	Ilford Works	Bombardier Transportation
ZK	Kilmarnock Works	Hunslet Barclay
ZN	Wolverton Works	Alstom
ZP	Horbury (Wakefield)	Bombardier Transportation

* = unofficial code.

ABBREVIATIONS

| DERA | Defence Evaluation & Research Agency |